A VERY SHORT,
FAIRLY INTERESTING AND
REASONABLY CHEAP BOOK ABOUT
QUALITATIVE RESEARCH

A VERY SHORT, FAIRLY INTERESTING AND REASONABLY CHEAP BOOK ABOUT QUALITATIVE RESEARCH

SECOND EDITION

DAVID SILVERMAN

Los Angeles | London | New Delhi
Singapore | Washington DC

Los Angeles | London | New Delhi
Singapore | Washington DC

SAGE Publications Ltd
1 Oliver's Yard
55 City Road
London EC1Y 1SP

SAGE Publications Inc.
2455 Teller Road
Thousand Oaks, California 91320

SAGE Publications India Pvt Ltd
B 1/I 1 Mohan Cooperative Industrial Area
Mathura Road
New Delhi 110 044

SAGE Publications Asia-Pacific Pte Ltd
3 Church Street
#10-04 Samsung Hub
Singapore 049483

Editor: Katie Metzler
Assistant editor: Anna Horvai
Production editor: Ian Antcliff
Copyeditor: Solveig Gardner Servian
Proofreader: Jennifer Hinchliffe
Marketing manager: Ben Griffin-Sherwood
Cover design: Wendy Scott
Typeset by: C&M Digitals (P) Ltd, Chennai, India
Printed and bound by : CPI Group (UK) Ltd,
    Croydon, CR0 4YY

MIX
Paper from
responsible sources
FSC
www.fsc.org
FSC® C013604

Published 2007, reprinted 2007, 2008 (twice), 2009,
2010 and 2011

Library of Congress Control Number: 2012931571

British Library Cataloguing in Publication data

A catalogue record for this book is available from
the British Library

ISBN 978-1-4462-5217-8
ISBN 978-1-4462-5218-5 (P)

Dedicated to my friends who are residents on the first and second floors of the Lady Sarah Cohen Home, London: Helen, Harry, Rita, Yvonne, Sam, Rachel, Rosalind, Hannah, Leon, Frank and many others. Thank you for what you have brought into my life.

Contents

Acknowledgments

Like many publishing ventures this book originated at a lunch with my then Editor. Although it was a very fine lunch, I was not initially receptive to Patrick Brindle's suggestion that I write a new book. Since my retirement from full-time teaching, I have concentrated upon the less demanding task of updating editions of my various textbooks. It was only later that I realised that the kind of provocative book Patrick wanted could be based on the lectures I had given over the past few years for the Qualitative Research Network of the European Sociological Association (ESA). Following a few emails between us, the present book is the product.

As Patrick requested, it is unashamedly based upon the formula used by Chris Grey in his book *A Very Short, Fairly Interesting and Reasonably Cheap Book about Studying Organisations* (Sage, 2005). I'm afraid I have stolen most of Chris's title as well as his idea to write a provocative introduction to my field in a non-textbooky kind of way. I hope he will forgive me.

Patrick has been a marvellous editor and critic. For this Second Edition, I am equally grateful for the advice and support of my new editor, Katie Metzler.

Many other people have been generous about reading and commenting on earlier drafts. I wish to thank Jay Gubrium, Alexa Hepburn, John Heritage, Celia Kitzinger, Ross Koppel, Doug Maynard, Anne Murcott, Jonathan Potter, Anne Ryen, Clive Seale and Gary Wickham. You have all inspired me, as have my friends and colleagues at the ESA Network.

At a personal level, I want to thank Sara Cordell for keeping my back in working order and my friends at The Nursery End NW8 (Leslie, Sol and John) for making my summers something to which I look forward. My children, Danielle and Andrew, have helped in ways they may not realise by challenging, in a loving spirit, the way I look at the world. Finally, I must thank my wife Gillian for her love and support.

Introduction to the Second Edition

This volume is intended as a lively, argumentative and personal pre-textbook – a taster for the issues involved in using qualitative methods. The most noticeable addition is a Glossary of Received Ideas. I have taken the name from the marvellous Dictionary of Received Ideas which appears at the end of Gustave Flaubert's nineteenth-century novel *Bouvard and Pecuchet* (2005). Like Flaubert, my aim is to debunk the accepted understandings of our time.

Most textbook glossaries seek to define terms which are central to their specific area. By contrast, my glossary lists terms which, although part of the conventional wisdom of qualitative research, to my mind, either mislead or misdirect us about what such research can offer.

The first edition of this book used many illustrative examples from art, literature and the theatre. However, in the second decade of the twenty-first century, I recognise that the Internet has transformed how we communicate. Consequently, this new edition adds considerable illustrative material from social media and other websites. I also make it clearer that this book will appeal most to those who primarily think of qualitative research as having an ethnographic character and use more examples from research studies to explain how we can pay attention to the sequential organisation of qualitative data.

Preface: Making a Space
for this Book

What do you imagine goes through the mind of authors as they write a book? Do you picture lonely geniuses or misguided bores who feel compelled to get into print knowing that their words will be misinterpreted or, still worse, ignored? Or do you think of the solid artisan who ploughs through masses of material in order to produce a work that will be acceptable to the maximum number of readers?

For the past decade or so, I have attempted to be such an artisan. The textbooks and edited readings I have produced (Silverman, 2010, 2011 and 2012) have aimed to be comprehensive and balanced. In pursuit of this aim, they have also been rather long. By contrast, this book is short and intentionally opinionated and partial.

We live in an age when qualitative research is often identified with open-ended interviews which aim to peer into people's inner experiences. By contrast, taking a constructionist perspective, this book favours using naturally-occurring data to study behaviour, positioning itself within certain kinds of ethnography and discourse and conversation analysis (CA).

This volume also lacks many traditional textbook features such as bullet-point lists, exercises and recommended readings. Even its glossary is meant to be provocative rather than a revision list of agreed definitions. So why on earth should you consider buying it?

If you want to be spoonfed or to find a quick read which you will dip into in order to scrape a pass on a research methods course, this is not the book for you. By contrast, my aim is to stimulate you by making you reconsider some assumptions that textbooks trade off.

This book comes with no claims to get you through a course. At best, an encounter with less conventional reading such as this may earn you some favour with teachers who are bored by pre-digested, textbook answers.

I know that university study increasingly seems like routine factory work in which you are required to produce a certain output while paying for the privilege. In such a context, there may be little time to look for intellectual stimulation. Why then should you put yourself out to venture beyond the minimum requirement?

To answer this question, in the next section I will explain why the mechanics of research might matter to you. After that, I will try to give you an idea why qualitative research has come to matter to me.

Why might research methods matter to you?

I want to answer this question concretely. Rather than give you an abstract argument, I would like you to think about some of the things you currently do and might do in the future. An important finding by qualitative researchers is that, rather than having one fixed conception of who we are, we all move between multiple identities (see Holstein and Gubrium, 1995; Rapley, 2004; and Silverman, 1987: Ch. 10). Think about three actual or possible identities: student, employee and citizen. Let us now consider the relevance of a knowledge of research methods for each identity.

If you are a student on a research methods course, it is quite likely that you will be asked to carry out a small-scale research project. If so, you may be tempted to seek simple 'cookbook' answers to your research question. But, if you are wiser, you will look for a textbook that tries to provide you with practical examples of actual research studies and offers hands-on experience of analysing data (these are the objectives of my own texts).

However, if you are a brighter student, you may crave to know more. This book seeks to offer you an entry into broader questions that many textbooks necessarily have to gloss over. For instance, what is the underlying logic of qualitative logic? And what are the key debates about its future direction? This book sets out an unashamedly partial answer to such questions.

Now imagine that you are employed in a job which requires you to keep up with research studies in your area. If so, you will need to be able to evaluate the credibility of any relevant findings. Or imagine you have to commission research. Now you will want to know what kinds of studies (quantitative, qualitative or multi-method) are appropriate and what kinds of methods and data-analysis will give you the results you are seeking. Once again, you will need to go beyond the limited horizons of a standard textbook.

Finally, we all are citizens. To a greater or lesser extent, we follow the news and want to take an informed position on current debates. With its focus on how people's interaction shapes phenomena as diverse as organisations and families, qualitative research gives you its own trademark understanding of everyday life. As I show in Chapters 1 and 4, by making mundane situations remarkable, qualitative research can bring into focus taken-for-granted forms of behaviour and open the way to new possibilities. As active citizens, this is information we need.

These are some of the identities you may move between. But what about my identity(ies)? How have they shaped what appears in the following pages?

◼◼◼ Why research methods matter to me

This section will involve a brief autobiographical account. Like many people, I stumbled into the subject of my first degree. I had studied economics at school and because that subject seemed to offer some potential for either a managerial or academic career, I applied to study for a degree in economics.

My first selection interview was spectacularly unsuccessful, in part because I had not properly prepared. When asked why I wanted to study economics at Nottingham University, I came up with the brilliant answer: 'because my best friend has applied for the same course'!

The rejection that followed made me rethink my strategy. Before the next interview, I read *The Economist* and followed its advice to read J.K. Galbraith's book *The Affluent Society* (1999). My comments on this book seemed to impress my next panel of interviewers and I was accepted to read for a BSc in Economics at the London School of Economics (LSE) with Industry and Trade as my special subject.

If I had followed my intended path, I might have ended up in industry or the British civil service. But fate intervened. Fed up with the rote teaching at my local secondary school, I convinced my parents to send me to a private tutorial college for the last six months of my pre-university studies. At this college, one of my teachers had newly graduated in sociology from LSE. It was one-to-one teaching and I was easily influenced. Almost overnight, I discovered sociology and the work of Karl Marx. Fortunately, the LSE BSc (Econ) was a relatively flexible degree and I was able to change my special subject.

In the 1960s, sociology at LSE was dominated by four figures: Tom Bottomore, Donald MacRae, David Glass and Robert McKenzie. From Bottomore and MacRae, I learnt that the main issues that mattered in British sociology arose in debates that grew out of nineteenth-century social theory in the work of Marx, Durkheim and Weber. Moreover, although Glass and McKenzie were researchers as well as theorists, the kind of research they favoured was mainly quantitative (demography and/or survey research). Indeed, the only research methods course around at LSE was on statistics – albeit very entertainingly taught by Claus Moser. Even the advanced methods course that I subsequently took at the University of California, Los Angeles (UCLA), for my MA in Sociology, was largely concerned with the design of quantitative research. Only a graduate seminar with Mel Dalton, author of a great piece of research on middle managers (Dalton, 1959), gave me a hint of what might be gained from more ethnographic work.

When I returned to the UK from UCLA, I began my research career with a study of the beliefs and values of junior 'white collar' workers. Influenced by sociological theories of class and social status deriving from the German sociologist Max Weber, I wanted to see if the way you perceived yourself was influenced by where you worked and by your future job prospects.

I used a structured interview schedule and my methodology was cast in the standard forms of quantitative research: an initial hypothesis, a two-by-two table and statistical tests (see Silverman, 1968). If I had completed this study, my future career might have taken a completely different path.

However, I started to have nagging doubts about the credibility of my research. Although I could manipulate my data so as to provide an apparently rigorous test of my hypotheses, this data was hardly 'raw' but mediated by various kinds of interpretive activities. Not the least of these arose in my administration of the interview schedule.

As I was interviewing my respondents, I was struck by the need to go beyond my questions in various, unforeseen ways in order to obtain the sort of answers I wanted. Perhaps, I thought, I hadn't pre-tested my questions properly. It was only much later that I learnt that how we make sense in conversations necessarily relies on everyday conversational skills that cannot be reduced to reliable techniques (see Rapley, 2004).

In any event, I abandoned this study and turned to organisation theory in a work that was to be both my Ph.D and a successful textbook (Silverman, 1970). The approach I used was influenced by a mid-twentieth century student of Weber, Alfred Schutz. Schutz's phenomenology of the everyday world was concerned with the structures of everyday life. It made an easy link, when in 1971–72, I was introduced to the study of the methods we all use in everyday life (ethnomethodology) by Aaron Cicourel, who was a visitor at Goldsmiths'. Ultimately, this led to a book (Filmer et al., 1972) which had a short-lived fame as an early British text sympathetic to ethnomethodology.

After a period immersed in organisation theory and philosophy, by the mid-1980s I had moved first into ethnomethodologically-inspired ethnography and then into CA. I spent the following decade exploring the uses of two contemporary social science theories. An ethnography of the personnel department of a public sector organisation (Silverman and Jones, 1976) was heavily influenced by Harold Garfinkel's (1967) ethnomethodology. And an analysis of literary texts (Silverman and

Torode, 1980) derived from Ferdinand de Saussure's (1974) semiotics (see Chapter 3). These studies confirmed my belief in the value of theoretically-informed research – a belief affirmed throughout the present text.

However, guiding principles tend to be double-edged. So, while we should assert their benefits, we should also be aware of their possible costs. Looking back on this early work, I now feel that it was a trifle over-theorised. Perhaps I had been so enthused by a newly discovered theory that I hadn't allowed myself to be sufficiently challenged, even surprised, by my data.

Such over-theorisation is an ever-present danger given that many social science disciplines still, I believe, run in fear of being discovered, like the fabled Emperor, without any clothes (for a valuable exception see Kendall and Wickham's, 1999, fine text on the practical research uses of Foucault's ideas). It is for this reason that what has been called the 'postmodern' period of experimental ethnographic writing comes under fire in Chapter 5 of this book.

In my later research, I tried to find a better balance between the theoretical 'armchair' and the empirical 'field'. In both an ethnography of hospital clinics (Silverman, 1987) and a conversation analytic study of HIV-test counselling (Silverman, 1997), I adopted a more cautious approach to my data, inductively establishing hypotheses, using the comparative method, and identifying deviant cases. In both studies, unlike my earlier work, I explored ways of making my research relevant to a wider, non-academic audience in a non-patronising way (see Chapter 4).

However, these later studies also derived from two related methodological assumptions present in my 1976 study of a personnel department. All three studies were based not on interviews but on naturally-occurring data (see Chapter 2). And all of them looked at how the participants talked to one another and focused on the skills they used and the local functions of what they did.

To sum up: research methods matter to me because my attempts to do worthwhile social research have brought me face to face with issues of principle that cut across both methodological and theoretical issues. This book is based on the lessons that research practice has taught me. It brings to the fore a number of positions that are implicit in my textbooks: a demand that qualitative research be methodologically inventive, theoretically alive and empirically rigorous.

This will give you some sense of 'where I am coming from'. However, this section would not be complete without a further autobiographical note. The first three chapters of this book make considerable use of the insights of the American sociologist Harvey Sacks. Sacks hardly figures in most contemporary courses on social theory or qualitative methodology. So why introduce him here?

In September 1964, after my first degree at the London School of Economics, I enrolled as a graduate student and teaching assistant in the Department of Sociology at the University of California, Los Angeles. By chance this coincided with Harvey Sacks's first set of lectures in this very department.

This might have offered an entirely new direction to my thought. Unfortunately, like nearly everybody else at the time, I had never heard about Sacks or his ideas. Moreover, given my background in the nineteenth-century theoretical sociology then fashionable in the UK, I probably would not have been interested anyway.

In June 1972, I met Sacks at the celebrated Edinburgh 'Ethnomethodology and Symbolic Interactionism' Conference. I remember the originality of what Sacks had to say (his lecture on dreams at that conference is not unlike the one reprinted in his published lectures, 1992, 2:512–20). I can also recall my ex-tutor at LSE, Ernest Gellner, noisily walking out in disgust from the hall during Sacks' talk. This culminated in a paper (Gellner, 1975) which Sacks's colleague, Emmanuel Schegloff, fairly dismisses as 'intellectually evasive' (Sacks, 1992, 2:x footnote 2).

My contact with Sacks's work was deepened by reading the photocopied versions of his lectures which circulated in the early 1970s. Sacks's inspiration allowed me to turn a full circle and to link my earlier theoretical interests with research practice. For Sacks re-opens a debate between ethnography and the nineteenth-century social theorist, Emile Durkheim (see also Gubrium, 1988). As an instance of this, you might try to guess the author of the following observation: 'Folk beliefs have honourable status but they are not the same intellectual object as a scientific analysis'.

If you guessed that the author was Emile Durkheim you were wrong, but also right in the sense that the observation above could be seen as true to Durkheim's dictum to treat 'social facts' as 'things'. Its actual author was the anthropologist (and Sacks's colleague) Michael Moerman (1974: 55).

Unlike Durkheim, ethnographers can take from Sacks a concern with understanding the 'apparatus' through which members' descriptions are properly (i.e. locally) produced. And this message has been taken on board by sociological ethnographers who, like Gubrium (1988), are centrally concerned with the descriptive process.

If a case can be made for Sacks's influence on (some) ethnography, it would appear, at first sight, difficult to make the same case for psychology.

After all, Sacks' analysis of the sequential organisation of conversation clearly reveals the inadequacies of any analyst's attempt to treat any utterance as an expression of someone's thoughts or, indeed, of any other apparently 'psychological' categories.

By contrast, in hearing how what they have just said is heard, speakers discover what they meant after they have spoken (for examples of this, drawn from AIDS counselling interviews, see Chapter 3). The critical implications of this for any psychology of, say, 'motive' are effectively underlined by Heritage (1974: 278–9), who reveals the inadequacies of any social psychology which tacitly treats commonsense as both a resource and a topic.

More recently, Derek Edwards, while reiterating Heritage's critique, has called for a psychology able 'to follow Sacks and look at how people use categories interactively' (1995: 582). Accepting that 'talk is action not communication', Edwards argues for a psychology which draws from Sacks and CA the assumption that 'no hearable level of detail that may not be significant, or treated as significant by conversational participants' (1995: 580).

The direction in which Edwards wants to take psychology clearly leads towards what has become called discourse analysis, or DA (see Potter, 2004). Writers who use the term DA have undoubtedly succeeded in showing the unlikely legacy that Sacks has given psychology. In a more obvious way, Sacks's contemporary influence also extends beyond CA and into ethnography whether located in Departments of Anthropology, Sociology or even Education (see Baker, 2004; and Freebody, 2003).

Despite this widespread influence, I suspect that the work of Harvey Sacks is often not even a minor component in contemporary social science courses. In part, no doubt, this reflects the unavailability of Sacks's lectures in published form until 1992. However, I guess that it also reflects either plain ignorance in the social science community or straightforward prejudice against 'another of those ethnos'.

Perhaps one way to make teaching Sacks more inviting to social scientists is to suggest that it might be a successful way to introduce more life into certain tired courses. Personally, I have never wanted to teach courses in social theory which, in my prejudiced way, I assume often contain empty syntheses, deadening critiques and the latest fashions in jargon. Certainly, the consumers of such courses respond as if this is was that they have been taught.

How invigorating then to introduce some of Sacks's examples on to such courses, such as 'the baby cried' and the Vietnam pilot (Silverman, 2011: 256–66). Talking through such examples with students must surely convey a little of the liveliness of social theory and its potential to deal with the world around them. Even more obviously, it is difficult to see how a course on research methodology could not gain by using material from Sacks. In this sense, I would demand that Sacks's writings should be basic reading on introductory classes in social theory and method.

As we shall see, Sacks recommended his method as a method anyone could use. In this sense, his lectures and other writings offer a toolbox rather than a museum exhibition. It is that toolbox which I hope to help make more widely known. Like my book on Sacks (Silverman, 1998), this work tries to reach a wider audience of scholars and students, particularly those who have never read Sacks, perhaps because they have assumed him to be 'one of those ethnos'.

To such an audience, I want to show that there is no sectarianism or petty-mindedness in Sacks's work. Instead, there is intellectual breadth and rigour. Whether or not we follow the path that Sacks sets out is perhaps less important than whether we respond to the questions that Sacks poses about social science. After almost forty years, they are, I believe still vitally important and still largely unanswered.

Like only Wittgenstein before him (see Chapter 1), and nobody since, Sacks had the ability to turn the apparently trivial into the gripping and insightful. As with other important thinkers, we keep Sacks's work vital by treating it as an inspiration or, more prosaically, as a toolbox. Indeed, the first three chapters of this book will have more than served their purpose if you are sufficiently stimulated to turn to Sacks's own writings to locate Sacks's legacy for yourself.

However, these biographical reflections should not mislead you into thinking that this is a book about Harvey Sacks or CA. What, then, is it about?

Organisation of this book

Having provided some sort of context to what I am doing here, now is the time to lay my cards on the table and to offer you a brief chapter-by-chapter synopsis of what follows. There has been much discussion about whether the skills needed to do good qualitative research can be taught directly or can only be learned through a long apprenticeship (Hammersley, 2004). This book is an attempt to hedge my bets in that debate. If my earlier textbooks suggested that direct teaching was sufficient (albeit aided by challenging exercises), the present volume attempts to convey some of the strategies and 'tricks' (see Becker, 1998) that I have learned through my own long apprenticeship in the trade.

As I have already noted, research is worthless unless it recognises its theoretical assumptions. So the first chapter of this book shows you the kinds of theoretically-based questions that qualitative researchers can effectively pose. Using photographs and extracts from social media as well as novels and plays, it reveals a tradition in which apparently routine activities can be made interesting and extraordinary things shown to have routine features.

Having seen what kinds of questions we can usefully ask, the next two chapters take you into nitty-gritty questions about the practice of qualitative research. It is a truism that data-collection methods can only be judged in relation to your research topic. However in Chapter 2, I try to show why, all things being equal, it usually makes sense in qualitative research to begin with data found in the everyday world. This means that what I call 'manufactured data' (e.g. including interviews and focus groups) should be used only as a last resort – particularly where a 'quick fix' is more important than in-depth knowledge of some phenomenon.

Whatever data collection method we use, we need to be less precious about the sanctity of our 'own' data. Indeed, secondary data analysis is a very important, if usually unacknowledged, method in qualitative research (see Corti and Thompson, 2004; Akerstrom et al., 2004; and Seale, 2011). Above all, it is the quality of our data analysis rather than the source of our data that ultimately matters. This means that time spent gathering data and doing literature reviews should be far *less* than the time given to analysing data and writing up your conclusions (see Silverman, 2010). Chapter 3 develops a strategy that I believe is a key to success in effective data analysis – avoiding appealing instances or examples and seeking out and analysing sequences in your data.

However, even if you do theoretically-inspired research with well-analysed data, people can still rightly ask 'so what?'. 'Pure' research is undoubtedly important but it should not blind us to the need to think through what contribution our research might make to 'society' and, indeed, what we mean by 'society'. Fortunately, as I show in Chapter 4, when properly conceived, qualitative research has a unique contribution to make to our understanding of how things in society work and how they can be changed.

Chapter 5 offers another way of answering the 'so what?' question. It asks in what ways qualitative research demands attention and claims to be of value. Unlike Chapter 4, I am concerned here with what qualitative research *is* rather than with what it *does*. I look at the claims that contemporary qualitative research makes about itself and find some of them to be misguided. I conclude by proposing an alternative aesthetic justification for our trade which reminds us of what we share with our quantitative cousins.

One final word is in order. I have emphasised that what follows reflects my own views. Although I am not wilfully controversial, I have fully taken up my Editor's invitation to speak my mind. So you should not be surprised if some of my arguments do not fit neatly with what you read elsewhere or with what your teachers tell you. Throughout my academic career I have never sought converts but cherished students with a sparkle in their eyes who can think for themselves. So if I have given you pause to reflect, I will not be dissatisfied, even if you end up taking positions quite opposed to mine.

Innumerable Inscrutable Habits: Why Unremarkable Things Matter

How do we see the world as the social science observer does? When you are studying your own society, much of what you see around you may seem 'obvious', existing as a mere unnoticed backdrop to your life. So it is tempting to take many things for granted. This temptation is supported by the swiftly changing images we absorb on the Internet and at the movies.

A method used by anthropologists can help us to slow down and look around rather more attentively. When we study familiar situations and events, we can try to make a mental leap and assume that we are observing the behaviour and beliefs of an unknown tribe. The shock in seeing the world as 'anthropologically strange' can help us find our feet.

This is not a new strategy. In the 1930s, some British anthropologists invented an innovative method to study everyday life. Instead of relying on their own observations or doing a quantitative social survey, they recruited 50 helpers through a letter in the press. These volunteers were asked to supply the following:

- a short report on themselves
- a description of their environment
- a list of objects on their mantelpieces (i.e. above their fireplaces)
- a day survey which provided an account of all that they saw and heard on the twelfth day of the month.

This form of research became known as Mass Observation. A contemporary newspaper reported the success of its first project:

> Six months after the first meeting, Mass Observation was able to organise a national survey of Britain on Coronation Day. A team of 15 reported on the procession, while from provincial towns and villages reports came in on local celebrations. From these 'mass observations', the first full-length book has been compiled. (*Manchester Guardian*, 14 September 1937)

Eventually Mass Observation had about 1500 active observers sending in day surveys. Here is one extract from a coal miner's description of his day reported by the same newspaper:

> At about 12.30 we received a visit from the deputy [i.e. supervisor]. He led off examining our place: it comprises about 50 yards of coalface. My eye follows where his Bull's-eye [miner's headlamp] flashes. He asks what I intend to do at this place, or what is required at that place. I differ with him on one point, and state my method. We argue for a short while, he from the point of view of a break-down in ventilation. We finally agree, and with a final Do this, and that, and that, and that! he leaves us. We are clothed in a pair of boots, stockings, and a pair of knickers, just around our middles. Perspiration rolls off us, our knickers are wet, of time we have no knowledge. If we continue as we are doing, we shall have a good shift. My six pints of water is being reduced, had better go steady.

Notice the degree of detail in this ordinary coal miner's observations. It is doubtless true that repeated viewings of a video of him at work with his mates would reveal more fine detail. Nonetheless, his account provides excellent observational data which stimulates further questions for investigation. For instance, what shapes his sense of 'a good shift'? Is his team paid by results or is he just concerned with doing his job well or in a happy spirit?

Let us move on from this thoughtful miner. In the rest of this chapter, I'll be using the technical term 'ethnography' rather than 'observation' to describe what many qualitative researchers do. No need to panic. Ethnography simply puts together two different words: 'ethno' means 'folk' or 'people', while 'graph' derives from 'writing'. Ethnography refers, then, to highly descriptive writing about particular groups of people.

In what follows, I'll try to find inspiration for the ethnographer in the work of writers and two photographers. I'll then circle back to the brilliant (sadly overlooked) programme for ethnography that the American sociologist Harvey Sacks laid out in his lectures at the University of California some 40 years ago.

Looking at photographs

Why consider photographs in a chapter on ethnography? A good answer is contained in the following extract from an exhibition of one photographer's work:

> Diane Arbus was committed to photography as a medium that tangles with the facts. Her devotion to its principles – without deference to any extraneous social, political or even personal agenda – has produced a body of work that is often shocking in its purity, in its bold commitment to the celebration of things as they are. (Arbus, 2005)

Like Arbus's photography, I believe that ethnography could have no better aim than 'to tangle with the facts ... without deference to any extraneous social, political or even personal agenda'. Today this view is contested by those who seek to advance their own political and personal agenda and question whether there can ever be any such things as 'facts'. In Chapter 5, I will discuss their arguments and show why I believe them to be misguided.

As I will try to demonstrate in this chapter, good ethnography, like Arbus's work, is 'often shocking in its purity, in its bold commitment to the celebration of things as they are'. Pursuing this line in a school essay written when she was 16 years old, Arbus wrote 'I see the divineness in ordinary things'.

What is involved in seeing ordinary things as 'divine'? In 1963, in a successful application for a Guggenheim Fellowship, Arbus wrote this brief note about her interests entitled 'American rites, manners and customs'. It was the inspiration for the title of this chapter:

> I want to photograph the considerable ceremonies of our present because we tend, while living here and now, to perceive only what is random and barren and formless about it. While we regret that the present is not like the past, we despair of its ever becoming the future, its innumerable inscrutable habits lie in wait for their meaning. I want to gather them like somebody's grandmother putting up preserves because they will have been so beautiful. (Arbus, 2005)

Arbus noted that we usually perceive the world around us as, among other things, 'random and formless'. About the same time, the Austrian social philosopher Alfred Schutz was writing that the everyday world is necessarily taken for granted. Setting aside these habits is the key to the ethnographic imagination.

What is involved in treating our 'innumerable inscrutable habits' as 'grandmother's preserves' which are 'beautiful' objects? Like the good ethnographer, Arbus wants us to see *the remarkable in the mundane*.

Let me illustrate this with one of her photographs (I will have to describe this photograph for you as I have been unable to obtain permission to reproduce it here. If you are interested, you can find it in the exhibition catalogue *Revelations*, mentioned earlier: Arbus, 2005). The photograph has the caption 'A family on their lawn one Sunday in Westchester, N.Y. 1968'. The photo shows a couple lounging on deck-chairs in the summer sun while their child plays behind them. In one sense, this could not be a more mundane setting. However, like all of Arbus's images, we are invited to construct many narratives from what we see. If you had the photograph in front of you, you might ask: 'Why is nobody speaking or even engaged in eye contact?' Each person seems self-absorbed. It is not clear whether the man in the picture is shielding his eyes from the sun or indicating a kind of despair.

But we do not need to psychologise our interpretation or to construct a closed narrative. Arbus also asks us to consider a basic ethnographic question: 'How far does routine family life depend on such silences?' Implicitly, she reminds ethnographers that this sort of question is only available from observation and hence unlikely to be generated by inter-views with family members.

So what is everyday family life actually like? The Israeli photographer Michal Chelbin is a good guide. Like Arbus, to whom she refers, her aim is to remind us of the remarkable in the mundane world. As she puts it:

> I am drawn to fantasy and fantastic elements in real environments ... Many viewers tell me that the world discovered in my images is strange. If they find it strange, it is only because the world is indeed a strange place. I just try to show that. (Chelbin, 2006: www.michal chelbin.com, Artist Statement)

A case in point is provided by a Chelbin photograph called 'Alicia, Ukraine 2005'.

Alicia stares out at us from the back of her car. Her gaze is ambiguous. Is she a child appealing for our help or a young adult asserting her inde-pendence both from us and the driver? Is the man in the front of the car her father or simply a taxi driver?

In a web commentary on these issues in 2006, Eve Wood suggests one answer:

> [R]evealed in this young woman's face is the haughtiness of youth, masking a deeper, more complex awareness of the difficulties in being so young and so beautiful. The girl seems to know something we do not and were we to discover her secret, she might come undone. (Wood, 2006: www.nyartsmagazine.com/index)

Does this photograph show, as Wood suggests, 'the haughtiness of youth' and a young woman who is aware of 'being so young and beautiful'?

Figure 1.1   Alici, Ukraine, 2005

Chelbin herself tells us of the danger of trying to construct a definitive account of her images. As she puts it: 'In my work, I try to create a scene where there is a mixture of straight information and riddles.'

To what extent should the ethnographer try to resolve such riddles? In one of his lectures, Harvey Sacks (1992) offers a case where you observe a car drawing up near you. A door opens and a teenage woman emerges and runs a few paces. Two other people (one male, one female) get out of the car. They run after the young woman, take her arms and pull her back into the car which now drives off.

Now clearly there are several different interpretations of what you have seen. Is this a kidnapping which you should report to the police? Or have you just seen a family row, in which case going to the police might turn you into a busybody?

Sacks expands on the problems this creates for the ethnographer:

> Suppose you're an anthropologist or sociologist standing somewhere. You see somebody do some action, and you see it to be some activity. How can you go about formulating who is it that did it, for the purposes of your report? Can you use at least what you might take to be the most conservative formulation – his name? Knowing, of course, that any category you choose would have the[se] kinds of systematic

problems: how would you go about selecting a given category from the set that would equally well characterise or identify that person at hand? (Sacks,1992, 1:467–8)

Sacks shows how you cannot resolve such problems simply 'by taking the best possible notes at the time and making your decisions afterwards' (1992, 1:468). Whatever we observe is impregnated by everyday assumptions and categories (e.g. kidnapper, family member). Rather than lazily employ such categories, Sacks tells us that the task of the ethnographer is to track which categories laypersons use and when and how they use them.

This raises a crucial question. To assemble information on laypersons' use of categories, do we need to get inside their heads (e.g. to interview them)? This is a big topic which comes to the fore in Chapter 2. At this stage, I will simply suggest that we can often find evidence of category use without needing to ask the people concerned. Think of the terms used by the Mass Observation coal miner to describe his working day. Or consider the rich texture of police reports of kidnappings and/or family disputes or of how they themselves interview witnesses and suspects. Such information constitutes fascinating material on how in real time, in situ, people collaboratively give meaning to their worlds.

The remarkable in the mundane

To look at the mundane world really closely can generate boredom. We think nothing is happening and prefer some 'action'. If we want to be a good ethnographer, the trick is to go beyond such boredom so that we can start to see remarkable things in quite mundane settings.

The early plays of Harold Pinter strike many people as boring in this sense. Take the opening scene of his play *The Birthday Party*. We are in the living-room of a house in a seaside town. Petey enters with a paper and sits at the table. He begins to read. Meg's voice comes through the kitchen hatch as follows:

Meg: Is that you, Petey?
        [Pause]
        Petey, is that you?
        [Pause]
        Petey?
Petey: What?
Meg: Is that you?

Petey: Yes, it's me.
Meg: What? [*Her face appears at the hatch*] Are you back?
Petey: Yes.
         (Pinter, 1976: 19)

'Where's the action here?', we might ask, particularly as much of the first act is composed of such everyday dialogues. Instead of launching us into dramatic events, Pinter writes a dialogue far closer to the tempo of everyday life. Because their expectations of 'action' have been disappointed, many people find the first act of *The Birthday Party* incomprehensible or just plain boring.

But recall Arbus's depiction of a silent family or Chelbin's photograph of a young woman silently looking out at us. In your own home, do your mother and father sometimes become obsessed in their own single projects and fail to listen to what others are saying? Perhaps Pinter, like Arbus, is pointing to the major role that mutual inattention plays in family life?

Moreover, this is not simply a psychological question about family dynamics. Pinter's opening scene reveals something basic to all interaction among families and otherwise. We all tacitly understand that we need to grab somebody's attention before we can raise a topic with them. As Sacks himself pointed out, this is most obvious for children who may struggle to gain a parent's attention and so learn not to launch into a conversation but always begin with something like:

'Mummy?' or
'You know what, Mummy?'

In the same way, in Pinter's dialogue, Meg works to get Petey's attention as Petey appears obsessed with reading his newspaper. But understanding mundane life extends beyond listening carefully to how people speak to one another. It also requires observation of fine detail.
Take the following extract from a weblog discussed by Hookway:

> *32-year-old male*: Things i've done recently: been to ikea, been to my local furniture shop, been to ikea again, been to ikea yes i know, ... again ... bought a rug, bought a lamp, bought a bigger lamp ... dug my lawn up, re-sown lawn, bought some shredded bark ... walked along the beach, moved the shelving unit from the lounge to the kitchen, paid for my flight, cut my hair ... had a performance review at work, asked for a pay rise, got laid, filed a years worth of bill ... thats all for now. (2008: 102–3)

Hookway treats this extract as an example of a purely descriptive blog of the kind which non-reflexively recounts the events of the day, from what the blogger:

> has eaten for breakfast to who they have seen that day. But the fine detail of this blog suggests even more. Look at how the blogger's use of a list of activities appears to give equal value to domestic tasks, work activities and sexual relationships. In a sense, his non-reflective style constitutes a very clear version of how he wants to be seen – cool, laid back, taking things as they come. (2008: 102–3)

Compare this to another blogger cited by Hookway:

> *36-year-old male*: I wish i had the magic to give Janine the life i stole from her. of all the people i've hurt in my life, it's her that i feel most dreadful about. she put so much trust and faith in me ... and i really loved her. i still do. yet i screwed her over and tore that wonderful heart in two. if only i had some way to make it so i'd never happened to her life ... if i could just patch up my era [*sic*] with a big sander bandaid ... so that it had been him that she'd met and not me. admittedly, i'd lose a part of my life that means a lot to me ... but i'd really rather never to have hurt her. and no matter how sorry i am, and how deeply i feel the grief, the apologies i give her can never unhurt her. (2008: 102–3)

As Hookway notes, this second blog is highly confessional and self-analytical. Yet, like the first blog, this man creates a version of how he wants to be seen – not only as remorseful but as someone who values another person more than himself.

Reading the second blog this way means moving on from our immediate response to it and asking how it achieves its effects. In the case of blogs, this involves close attention to the mundane detail of how people present themselves.

But, contrary to blogs and soap operas, everyday life is not just about 'relationships'. It also involves navigating a material world and the objects within it. Take a passage from Paul Auster's novel *Moon Palace*. It is from the point of view of a student who has been employed as a companion by a blind man called Effing:

> As soon as we got outside, Effing would begin jabbing his stick in the air, asking in a loud voice what object he was pointing at. As soon as I told him, he would insist that I describe it for him. Garbage cans, shop windows, doorways: he wanted me to give a precise account of

these things, and if I couldn't muster the phrases swiftly enough to satisfy him, he would explode in anger. 'Dammit, boy', he would say, 'use the eyes in your head! I can't see a bloody thing, and here you're spouting drivel about 'your average lamppost' and 'perfectly ordinary manhole covers'. No two things are alike, you fool, any bumpkin knows that. I want to see what we're looking at, goddammit, I want you to make things stand out for me! (Auster, 1990: 117)

The blind man, Effing, understands the importance to sighted people of using 'the eyes in your head'. He insists that his sighted companion describes in detail the ordinary things whose existence the latter finds plain obvious.

Such an attention to how we navigate the objects around us is also a concern of the novelist Rachel Cusk. As a reviewer of her novel *Arlington Park* remarks:

Her writing takes nothing for granted, applying itself to the most mundane objects and moments – the act of parking a car, the look of an untidy bedroom or a fashion boutique – with an attentiveness that again and again provides that primal joy of literature: the sense of things being seen afresh. (James Lansdun, *Guardian*, 9 September 2006)

'Things being seen afresh' is also the hallmark of good ethnographic description. To do ethnography you don't need to enjoy reading novels of this kind. As an alternative, you might look below the surface of blogs and ask how they achieve their effects. At the very least, you will need to appreciate the value (and, ultimately, the beauty) of the fine details of mundane existence.

But ethnography is not only about seeing remarkable things in everyday situations. It also asks us to see the *mundane* elements of *remarkable* events and contexts.

The mundane in the remarkable

Michal Chelbin has described how people view her photographs as follows:

Many viewers tell me that the world discovered in my images is strange. If they find it strange, it is only because the world is a strange place. I just try to show that.' (Chelbin, 2006: www.michalchelbin. com, Artist Statement)

Full address: http://www.michalchelbin.com/popup.php?m=1

Figure 1.2   Mickey and Amir, Russia, 2004

She has recently observed circus artistes backstage in a number of European countries. The photograph of Mickey and Amir is taken from this period.

The Mickey and Amir photograph clearly takes us into a different realm from the earlier image of Alicia in a car. Although the latter generates many puzzles, it shows a quite familiar scene. But a boy with a chimpanzee is not at all routine, particularly as the chimpanzee has his arm around Amir's shoulder, looking, for all the world, like a human parent or sibling.

Eve Wood comments that this image is

> overtly eccentric in the same way a Diane Arbus photograph captures a moment of unique tenderness ... Yet, within this exquisite oddness is a quiet harbor, as the chimp poses alongside the little boy like an old Vaudevillian friend. (Wood, 2006, www. nyartsmagazine.com/index)

Whether we see the boy and the chimp posed like variety hall colleagues or family members, Chelbin's photograph reminds any observer that we need not focus purely on the unfamiliar elements in apparently extraordinary situations. Maybe we should not assume that chimpanzees are merely quaint animals. Perhaps we can understand ourselves better in observing how we interact with others.

An experience I had in South East Asia many years ago helps to illustrate this point. I had managed to cadge an air ticket via Bali from people who had invited me to speak at a conference in Australia. Against my better judgment, I went on an excursion to a place advertised as 'a village where natives live as they did hundreds of years ago'.

On arrival, I discovered a number of thatched huts which all looked surprisingly new. In these huts, local craftsmen could be seen working on various artefacts. Attracted by the sound of Indonesian *gamelan* music coming from such a hut, I entered. Sure enough a Balinese man was making musical instruments. Surprisingly, given this purported trip back in time, he also was using a modern sound system to play *gamelan* tunes. He looked up and noticed me moving around to the music while carefully looking around his hut and said in perfectly understandable English: 'I think you are anthropologist'!

This episode served to remind me of the limits of that form of tourism which always wants to find something new, exotic and different. In some ways, this kind of upmarket tourism is just as blinkered as the more downmarket British or German tourists who go to Spain in order to live exactly the same life as at home but in the sunshine. Unlike them, I had sought something unfamiliar, only to discover something very routine – a kind of Balinese theme park. Moreover, rather than being a passive object of my gaze, this Balinese craftsman had looked back at me and quickly summed up my own interests.

As before, some literary examples will illustrate the mundane elements we can find in odd situations. Beckett's short play *Happy Days* (1961) certainly has a most bizarre setting. Two middle-aged characters, Winnie and her husband Willy, are buried up to their necks in sand on a huge, featureless, unpopulated beach. Nearly all the dialogue comes from Winnie.

If we watch and listen carefully, once again very mundane elements emerge from this bizarre setting. Next to where her head emerges from the sand, lies Winnie's handbag. It turns out to contain the routine artefacts that most women carry around with them. As night falls, Winnie reaches into her bag and takes out a comb and a toothbrush and, like most of us before bedtime, brushes her teeth and combs her hair. Before this happens, we see that, like Arbus's and Pinter's couples, stilted communication is the order of the day. For many of Winnie's remarks are addressed to her husband, who lies also buried in the sand a few yards away. But, like Pinter's Petey, Willy is self-obsessed and only speaks after several attempts by his wife to engage him in conversation.

Extraordinary episodes in real life usually contain such mundane features. The author Ford Madox Ford tells an anecdote of a meeting between the two great men of early twentieth-century literature, Marcel Proust and

James Joyce, at a dinner party at the Hotel Majestic in Paris in 1922. Proust and Joyce faced one another surrounded by their admirers. They were invited to converse. Eventually, they did. Below, I have translated from the French the substance of what they said:

M. Proust: 'As I said in my book *Swann's Way*, which no doubt you have read, Sir ...'
Mr Joyce: [giving a tiny vertical jump on his chair seat] 'No, Sir.'
    [Pause]
    'As Mr Bloom says in my *Ulysses*, which, Monsieur, you have doubtless read ...'
M. Proust: [giving a slightly higher vertical jump on *his* chair seat] 'Oh no, Sir.'
    (Davenport-Hines, 2006: 40–1)

Ford reports that a difficult silence ensued between the two men, broken only when Proust mentioned his many symptoms of illness. Joyce compared his symptoms eagerly. So, far from an extraordinary conversation between two literary giants, their audience heard mundane talk between two hypochondriacs!

But remarkable events are not always humorous like this. The Italian writer Primo Levi's particular genius was in depicting the mundane features of an unthinkable, horrific event – the Holocaust. Here is his account of how people prepared the night before being sent on a cattle truck to a concentration camp:

> All took leave from life in the manner which most suited them. Some praying, some deliberately drunk, others lustfully intoxicated for the last time. But the mothers stayed up to prepare the food for the journey with tender care, and washed their children and packed the luggage and at dawn the barbed wire was full of children's washing hung out in the wind to dry. Nor did they forget the diapers, the toys, the cushions and the hundred other small things which mothers remember and which children always need. Would you not do the same? If you and your child were going to be killed tomorrow, would you not give him something to eat today? (Levi, 1979: 21)

And this is how he describes the arrival at the camp:

> Everything was as silent as an aquarium, or as in certain dream sequences. We had expected something more apocalyptic: they seemed simple police agents. It was disconcerting and disarming. Someone

dared to ask for his luggage: they replied, 'luggage afterwards'. Someone else did not want to leave his wife: they said, 'together again afterwards'. They behaved with the calm assurance of people doing their normal duty every day. (Levi, 1979: 25)

As Hannah Arendt has argued, in some respects, the most mundane features of the horrific events of the Holocaust are the most harrowing. Indeed, Claude Lanzmann's brilliant documentary called *Shoah* is particularly effective because of its focus on the detail of the extermination process. It features interviews with middle-level staff of German railways who tell Lanzmann the routine methods used for charging the Nazi government for transporting people to the camps – an issue still very much to the fore in recent years when the French railways (SNCF) were sued for profiting from similar transports.

The following passage from Primo Levi deals with one mundane aspect of life for those who survived the initial selections in the concentration camp. It shows the potentially fatal link between being sent to the camp hospital and losing one's only eating implement:

> The nurses ... make huge profits from the trade in spoons ... it is a law that although one can enter Ka-Be [the camp hospital] with one's spoon, one cannot leave with it. At the moment of release ... the healthy patient's spoon is confiscated by the nurses and placed on sale in the Market. Adding the spoons of the patients about to leave to those of the dead and selected, the nurses receive the gains of the sale of about fifty spoons every day. On the other hand, the dismissed patients are forced to begin work again with the initial disadvantage of half a ration of bread, set aside to acquire a new spoon ...

> We now invite the reader to contemplate the possible meaning in the Lager of the words 'good' and 'evil', 'just' and 'unjust'; let everybody judge, on the basis of the picture we have outlined and of the examples given above, how much of our ordinary moral world could survive on this side of the barbed wire. (Levi, 1979: 91–2)

Levi shows us how the horror of the concentration camp can best be understood by appreciating its most mundane elements (e.g. acquiring an eating implement like a spoon). However, such an essentially ethnographic gaze demands very careful observation. As Paul Auster's blind man's companion comments:

> I realised that I had never acquired the habit of looking closely at things, and now that I was being asked to do it, the results were

dreadfully inadequate. Until then, I always had a penchant for generalising, for seeing the similarities between things rather than their differences. (Auster, 1990: 117)

Recognising such differences is a useful watchword for the ethnographer. This was also understood by the early twentieth-century German philosopher of language, Ludwig Wittgenstein. A student of his remembers the following comment that Wittgenstein made about what mattered to him:

Hegel seems to me to be always wanting to say that things which look different are really the same. Whereas my interest is in showing that things which look the same are really different. (Drury, 1984: 157)

Wittgenstein's German-speaking contemporary, Walter Benjamin, seems to have been equally fascinated by differences between apparently trivial objects. Hannah Arendt tells us that 'Benjamin had a passion for small, even minute things. For him the size of an object was in inverse ratio to its significance ... The smaller the object, the more likely it seemed that it could contain in the most concentrated form everything else' (1970: 11–2).

Apparently, Benjamin carried around with him notebooks containing quotations from daily living which he regarded as 'pearls' or 'coral: 'On occasion he read from them aloud, showing them around like items from a choice and precious collection' (1970: 45).

Ethnography in the Internet age

Nowadays, unlike Benjamin, rather than use a personal notebook, we might post our observations on our Facebook wall or on an internet bulletin board, chat room or, as we saw earlier, post a blog. In the past twenty years, the Internet has transformed the way we look at the world. Not only do we have access to more information than ever before but social network sites allow us instant communication with old and new friends and colleagues. Robert Kozinets has sketched the scope of this change and its potentially liberating consequences:

In 1996, there were approximately 250,000 sites offering published content to the online world of approximately 45 million global users, who were mainly located in North America and Western Europe. In 2009, there are now over 1.5 billion users of the Internet around the world accounting for 22 per cent of the world's population. Moreover, these users are not passively consuming published content as they were in 1996 – they are actively communicating with one another. They are reaching out to form, express and deepen their social alliances and affiliation. (2010: 2)

As Annette Markham notes, such active communication allows us to establish many more identities and to move freely between them:

> As I write … various programs on my computer and my smart phone collaborate to present a snapshot of not only my world, but also my understanding of *the* world. I filter news, I follow links sent by friends, and I follow random or not-so-random paths of information to build my knowledge of the world. I scan and contribute to various social networks. Each context is unique, each post authored by a slightly different version of 'me' and targeted to slightly different audiences. I'm a cook posting new recipes. I'm a photographer. I could be a methodologist, but I could also be a birdwatcher, a player of multiplayer online games, a dominatrix in an avatar-based social space, or a microcelebrity, known for my acerbic reviews of YouTube viral videos or my roles in amateur porn video. I could have a team of ghostwriters enacting my identity through Twitter if I were important enough. (2011: 121)

Yet, despite these optimistic accounts, it is still worth asking how far the new technologies of the Internet have supported the ethnographic gaze with its interest in mundane, routine activities. Certainly, we are now flooded by information. But what kind of information?

Take the rolling news stories available on many websites. How often do such stories allow us to grasp the texture of events in all their messy detail? Or does such news often report 'pseudo-events' like movie openings: 'occurrence(s) contrived purely to accrue publicity, something which would not happen if cameras were not pointed at it' (Andrew Mueller, 'Defining Moment' *Ft.Com Magazine*, 14/15 August 2010: 46).

Internet coverage of reality TV programmes like *Big Brother* is a case in point. As Michael Bywater acidly points out, the media will

> write about [*Big Brother*] at length, despite saying that they aren't going to write about it because it's a flop, which they are saying because nothing will make people watch a reality TV show more assiduously than being told it's a flop, so it won't be a flop after all. (2007: 119)

Even when we obtain information about real events, what do we really learn from it? Does the endless coverage of the trials of Michael Jackson's doctor and of Amanda Knox (see Box 1.1) do any more than reinforce our preconceptions about celebrities and 'dangerous' women?

Box 1.1   Celebrities in the headlines

Will Foxy spare a thought for the Kerchers?

(Daily Mail, 7 October 2011)

Amanda Knox 'Overwhelmed' as She Returns Home to Seattle

(*Good Morning America – Wednesday, 5 October 2011*)

Michael Jackson Doctor called Girlfriend as MJ died

(www.mtv.com – 4 October 2011)

Michael Jackson slept with a doll

- Bedroom full of baby pics
- Drugs bottles litter room

(*Sun*, 7 October 2011)

The history of Michael Jackson's face

(www.anomalies-unlimited.com)

The ethnographic gaze wants to tease out, say, the routine organisation of the courtroom or how lawyers use typifications of doctors and young women. By contrast, such rolling news usually only helps us to understand extraordinary events by unreflective use of stereotypes of 'good' and 'evil' people. As Judith Flanders observes:

> Sex sells; death sells. Add the two together, throw in a violent woman, and you have newspaper heaven. The nickname 'Foxy Knoxy' created the image of a young middle class woman who enjoyed sex. From there it was a short step to suggesting that her sexuality made her deviant; then, because she was deviant, she was, in all probability, a murderer too. (The Women's Room, *Guardian*, 7 October 2011)

To make matters worse, the age of social media has established that nothing is significant unless it is interactive. This means that when, say, the BBC website reports a news event, it always appends a request: if you are there, let us know what you are seeing and what you think of it. Even if you weren't there, news websites always make it clear that they welcome your views as in this example noted by Bywater:

> BBC website 'Have Your Say' section asks for 'Toronto Air Crash: Your Reaction'. (2007: 26)

As Bywater comments, what are you expected to say about such a disaster? Perhaps 'Great! Loved it!' Equally, think how often the unfortunate people who have been involved in disasters are invited to answer the question 'How do you feel?'.

Such 'interactivity' is the very opposite of the ethnographer's gaze. It invites participants to trot out the socially appropriate response while blocking insights into the social organisation of apparently extraordinary events. Why is it that, when someone dies in tragic circumstances, their family has to make a statement requesting 'privacy'? It is because now, in the era of interactivity, nothing can be private. We all have an appetite for others' grief – viewing it, enjoying it, commenting on it and so on.

By contrast, the ethnographer's gaze is fixed on social organisation. Rather than interview relatives, we might turn to how the fact of 'death' is accomplished. As David Sudnow (1968) showed, the routines of nurses' shifts may mean that, if someone dies on a hospital ward in the early morning, a night nurse may have an incentive to overlook it in order to avoid delaying her return home. In this way, the patient's 'death' does not happen until it is discovered by the day shift.

Or, to take a more extraordinary example, after President Kennedy was shot, he was taken to a Dallas hospital with, according to contemporary accounts, half of his head shot away. My hunch is that if you or I were to arrive in a casualty department in this state, we would be given a cursory examination and then recorded as 'dead on arrival' (DOA). Precisely because they were dealing with a President, the staff had to do more than this. So they worked on Kennedy for almost an hour, demonstrating thereby that they had done their best for such an important patient. In both cases, then, the ethnographer's instinct is to find ordinary features in extraordinary events.

I have been arguing that certain aspects of internet communication may make it particularly hard for us to adopt the ethnographer's gaze. It is worth noting that this does not conflict with the suggestion that internet material can be a great source for ethnographic research (Kozinets, 2010; and Markham, 2011).

Overcoming four contemporary cultural impulses

At this point of the chapter, it makes sense to take stock. I have suggested that the ethnographer's gaze demands two things: being able to locate the mundane features of extraordinary situations and to identify what is remarkable in everyday life. Do not worry if you are having trouble in readjusting your gaze in the way I am suggesting. Even if you are familiar with the relatively obscure writers, philosophers and photographers I have been considering, your path will not be easy. In part, this is because contemporary cultures, aided by new information technologies, incite us to avoid looking at the world in the way that ethnographers do. Let me explain a little of what I mean.

Precisely because the everyday world is so familiar, it presents itself to us as an undifferentiated, bland sameness. This apparent sameness is reinforced by popular culture's emphasis on dramatic incident. This means that the aspirant ethnographer must resist many of the messages and desires repeated when we are entertained by diverting sounds and images.

What follows is a brief sketch of what I take to be important messages that we find around ourselves in the contemporary world. To test out the accuracy of what I am saying, you can think about what media products appeal to you (e.g. music, movies, books, computer games, internet chat rooms) and consider how apposite my comments are.

1. The desire for everything to be the same

This may seem like a strange description of contemporary culture. After all, don't we all have very different tastes? Take our taste in movies. Some people like action movies. Others like romantic comedies or detective stories. Aren't these quite different genres?

Yes and no. The content and structure of these movies may be different but they are all *genre* movies. This means that, even before we enter the cinema or view a DVD, we have distinct expectations about the kind of characters we are going to see and the direction the plot will take. So, for instance, a romantic comedy is likely to feature two lovers whose path to happiness is beset by a number of complicating incidents and characters. Indeed, such genre features are so basic to storytelling that, in the 1930s, the Russian literary critic Vladimir Propp worked out that practically all Western stories can be reduced to half a dozen or so basic structures (see Silverman, 2011: 76–8).

However, it is a mistake to assume that such recurrent structures are limited to the stories we find in movies and books. For instance, think of media reports of real-life tragic accidents and disasters. From a brief study of such reports, I can reveal a seemingly unvarying social fact: everyone who dies tragically has led a very special life. Nobody who dies in tragic circumstances is without remarkable features. If you don't believe me, search your local newspaper or the Web for a relevant report and see for yourself. When you do so, you will become an ethnographer who seeks recurrent, mundane elements in apparently extraordinary events and situations.

What is going on in these reports is the production of stories that contain the kind of basic genre features that Propp identified. So we find heroes and heroines overcome by dramatic or evil people and events despite the best attempts of their helpers. Curiously, while these reports present themselves as giving us 'news', in large part, they recurrently repeat the same things.

The same sort of issues arise in celebrity interviews. Take the BBC TV coverage of the Young Musician of the Year competition. In recent years, less and less of the actual performances by these fine artists is transmitted. Instead, we get pre- and post-performance interviews with the players. Instead of hearing music, we learn about the players' hobbies and how they 'felt' during their performance.

Or take interviews with authors – perhaps the upmarket aspect of this genre. Rarely do you find questions about writing as literature or as participating in a particular literary tradition. Instead, you find the same two questions:

- How do you start writing every day?
- How do your stories relate to your own life?

This attempt to reduce artworks to their authors' beliefs and experiences reflects what the novelist Ian McEwan has called 'the exultation of the subjective'. McEwan then goes on to point out some sensible rules for reading (and writing) fiction:

> [Y]our not 'liking' the characters is not the same as your not liking the book; you don't have to think that the central character is nice; the views of the characters don't have to be yours, and are not necessarily those of the author; a novel is not always *all about you* [i.e. the author]. (*Guardian*, Letters, 7 April 2007)

A recent British TV interview with the American novelist Philip Roth ignored McEwan's request to focus on the novel itself rather than its author. The interviewer, Mark Lawson, tried to get Roth to relate his latest novel (*Everyman*) about one person's illnesses and death to Roth's own experiences of illness. Roth became more and more exasperated by this line of questioning and eventually responded ironically:

> Yes. Everything actually happened that way to me. In fact, it happened in the very same words. All I had to do was to write them down.

Roth's joke at Lawson's expense reminds me of an anecdote by the great American songwriter of the 1940s, Sammy Kahn, about a question he was often asked: 'When you write a song, what comes first – the words or the music?' To which Kahn replied: 'No, not the words or the music – first comes the phone call!'

Kahn's joke has a serious significance. It shows that our concern for the 'experience' of creative artists neglects a central ethnographic issue: how their extraordinary products are located in the social organisation of artistic practice (in Kahn's case, how the composition of a new song arose from a particular commission).

This means that interviewers' search for an artist's 'inspiration' in personal events serves to displace an ethnographic interest in literary production. As Pico Lyer has pointed out, such interviews now seem more central than the novels themselves. As he puts it: 'In the age of celebrity culture ... a writer is encouraged to talk *about* books more than to *write* them, and to turn herself into a commodity the books promote (rather than the other way round).'

He comments on an aggressive answer by the novelist and critic Susan Sontag to an interviewer's question about her life: 'I heard in her response the last gasp, perhaps, of the last generation that grew up with a sense of books, and not the chatter about them, the TV profiles or the Google listings, really mattering or having the power to speak' (*Guardian*, Review, 8 July 2006).

The second impulse which now follows underlines my earlier point that our desire for satisfying, familiar stories is not limited to novels and movies but extends to how we ordinarily observe the world around us.

2. The desire for a good story

> Two in three motorists admit to 'rubber-necking' – slowing down to have a good look at accidents as they pass – and as many as 10% have actually stopped so they can get a better view, while one in 20 has had a crash while rubbernecking, a survey by breakdown company Green Flag found. (Report in the *Guardian*, 2006)

Why do we tend to 'rubberneck' in this way? An answer was provided in the 1960s in a classic lecture by Harvey Sacks. Sacks argues that 'experience' is not something that just exists inside our heads. Instead, society grades our 'rights' to have an 'experience' depending on whether it is first- or second-hand. This means that the force of a story depends on the extent to which the storyteller can claim to have 'experienced' the events narrated.

Actually seeing a motorway pileup provides far more 'authenticity' than simply passing on a TV report of the same event. Hence the prevalence of rubbernecking.

So the desire to own an experience can actually be associated with death on the roads!

This has a clear implication for ethnography. When we return from the 'field', do we behave like upmarket tourists using our first-hand rights to an 'experience'? If so, our accounts will probably focus upon dramatic incidents involving strange people. Alternatively, have we been able to understand the routines of behaviour in our setting and to appreciate the similarities, as well as the differences, between the people we have been studying and ourselves?

3. The desire for speed and action

> Ian McEwan's *Saturday* was a recent favourite, such a feat to condense the action into a single day. ('My Media', Pippa Haywood, *Media Guardian*, 27 March 2006)

Haywood's account of her response to McEwan's novel seems plausible. As she says, while in most novels the action extends over months or even years, the events in McEwan's book occur on a single day.

But why should it be difficult to think that there is not enough action in any one day to provide a developed narrative? If you have followed my argument so far, the answer should be clear to you by now. In popular culture, everyday life is not perceived to contain enough 'incident'. By contrast, novelists such as Ian McEwan, like the good ethnographer, can take the events of one day and start to unwind massively complex worlds. Indeed, a whole day can be quite a long timespan. Analysing in detail a brief incident or conversation may turn out to offer a key to understanding everyday interaction in our field settings.

4. The desire for closure

I have been arguing that popular culture appeals to our desire to be diverted by exciting images and predictable storylines. This is not something new. Centuries ago, even though the technologies of production and consumption were very different, popular culture still satisfied the same impulses. Think about the appeal of stories about public executions in the eighteenth century, or how fairytales have hooked children for many centuries. As with most modern-day narratives, we know we can look beyond the twists in the tale to a satisfying ending where all the loose ends of the plot are tied together.

Think of the conventions of an Agatha Christie detective story in which all the suspects are ultimately grouped together in a room so that our brilliant detective can explain everything and, thereby, identify the murderer. Or take Alfred Hitchcock's famous film *Rear Window* in which a man in his wheelchair observes a crime through his apartment window. A whole story unfolds as James Stewart watches what is going on in a nearby apartment.

But how realistic is this? Are stories ever really so neat, so immediately viewable? Here is a contrasting view in Andrew Cowan's recent novel about a private detective:

> In all the years I have worked as a professional snoop ... I've rarely seen anything so tidily framed, so readily interpreted ... Most of the time I see only fragments – glimpses and snatches, parts of pictures, parts of stories ... It's a grainy, partial view, and mine is not a vivid existence ... but one that requires a great deal of patience, diligence and caution. (Cowan, 2006: 67–9)

To my mind, the sociologist most conscious of the need for such 'patience, diligence and caution' was Harvey Sacks. What follows are a few snippets from Sacks that illuminate this approach. They show that while Sacks is usually associated with the highly specialist approach called 'conversation analysis' (CA), his published lectures are a goldmine for ethnographers.

Sacks on detail

> [P]ursue truth, not rarity. The atypical can fend for itself. ... And very often, when we are looking over several common truths, holding them next to one another in an effort to feel again what makes them true, rarities will mysteriously germinate in the charged space between them. (Baker, 1997: 24)

For Sacks, like the essayist Nicholson Baker, rarity was never the point. The mysterious germination of rarities out of the familiar to which Baker refers is matched by Schegloff's observation that, in Sacks' work, 'previously unsuspected details were critical resources in [seeing] what was getting done in and by the talk' (Sacks, 1992, 1:xviii).

Sacks rejected 'the notion that you could tell right off whether something was important' (1992, 1:28). He uses the case of biology to show how the study of an apparently minor object ('one bacterium') can revolutionise our knowledge.

Why assume, for instance, that you need to look at states and revolutions when 'it's possible that some object, for example proverbs, may give an enormous understanding of the way humans do things and the kinds of objects they use to construct and order their affairs' (1992, 1:28)?

For instance, if you are challenged about your actions, one effective response may be to say 'everyone does don't they?' (1992, 1:23). Here the appeal to 'everyone' in this proverb works as a rhetorical device rather than a statistical claim. As such, it serves to limit your accountability for your act because such behaviour can be seen as 'general'.

Similarly, invoking a proverb (e.g. 'better late than never') is a powerful conversational move for reasons quite unconnected with whether the proverb is 'true' or even 'true in this instance'. Sacks notes that using a proverb as a conversational opener typically produces a token of agreement from the hearer. In this respect, it may be yet another effective pickup device.

By contrast, people who fail to agree with an invoked proverb will find that the conversation is abruptly terminated by the proverb reciter. This may be because proverbs are usually treated as unchallengeable and therefore as something any conversationalist will know (1992, 1:25). Hence challenging a proverb is an effective means of resisting an intended pickup by means of a proverb statement.

Like Sacks, Baker refuses to accept the prevailing version of the 'big' question. Baker's (1997) essays on apparently tiny topics from the history of punctuation to the aesthetics of nail-clippings and old library index cards may infuriate some readers. However, behind such seeming trivia lies what I take to be a serious intent – to seek clarity and insight by closely examining apparently 'small' objects. No reader of Sacks's lectures can doubt that, forty years earlier, social scientists had been invited to walk down this very path, eschewing empty accounts of 'big' issues in favour of elegant analyses which make a lot out of a little.

Sacks was convinced that serious work paid attention to detail and that, if something mattered, it should be observable. For instance, in a fascinating passage, Sacks noted the baleful influence on sociology of the American social psychologist G.H. Mead's proposal that we need to study things which are not available to observation (e.g. 'society', 'attitudes'). As Sacks comments:

> But social activities are observable, you can see them all around you, and you can write them down. The tape recorder is important, but a lot of this can be done without a tape recorder. If you think you can see it, that means we can build an observational study. (1992, 1:28)

However, ethnographers' praiseworthy attention to detail rarely satisfied Sacks's rigorous methodological demands. In particular, it is dangerous to take for granted what it is we appear to be 'seeing'. As Sacks says:

> In setting up what it is that seems to have happened, preparatory to solving the [research] problem, do not let your notion of what could conceivably happen decide for you what must have happened. (1992, 1:115)

Here Sacks is telling us that our 'notion of what could conceivably happen' is likely to be drawn from our unexamined knowledge as members of society. Instead, we need to proceed more cautiously by examining the methods members use to produce particular activities as observable and reportable 'events'. This means that people should not be seen as 'coming to terms with some phenomenon' (1992, 1:437) but as actively *constituting* it. Let us look at a few of Sacks's examples of this.

Speed on the roads

Take the phenomenon of 'speeding' – how does one know one is speeding? One solution is to look at your car's speedometer. However, another well-used method is to compare your movement relative to other traffic. And 'traffic' is a phenomenon that is actively organised by road users. As Sacks suggests:

> [P]ersons can be seen to clump their cars into something that is 'a traffic', pretty much wherever, whenever, whoever it is that's driving. That exists as a social fact, a thing which drivers do ... [so] by 'a traffic' I don't mean that there are some cars, but there is a set of cars that can be used as 'the traffic', however it's going; those cars that are clumped. And it is in terms of 'the traffic' that you see you're driving fast or slow. (1992, 1:437)

Sacks is arguing here that, rather than being a natural fact, 'the traffic' is a self-organising system, in which people adjust their speed by reference to how they define 'the traffic'. The traffic thus serves as a metaphor for how social order is constructed by reference to what can be inferred. It also shows how the ability 'to read other people's minds' (in this case, the minds of other drivers) is not a psychotic delusion but a condition for social order. For Sacks, then, 'traffic' and 'speed' are not natural facts but locally assembled phenomena. The selfsame features can be seen in medical interviews, where what is 'normal' is attended to by doctors on the basis of their elicitation of what is normal for *you* (Sacks, 1992, 1:57–8).

Observing crime on the street

For Sacks, police officers face the same kind of problem as the Shetland Islanders that Erving Goffman studied for his classic ethnography *The Presentation of Self in Everyday Life* (1959). The problem that police officers share with us all is: how are we to infer moral character from potentially misleading appearances? To solve this problem, police 'learn to treat their beat as a territory of normal appearances' (Sacks, 1972: 284) so that they can treat slight variations in normal appearances as 'incongruities' worthy of investigation. Throughout, policemen, like criminal lawyers, judges and juries, work with the assumption of the appearances of what David Sudnow has called typifications of 'normal' crimes.

The implication of Sacks's comments is that the study of how members of society use categories should make ethnographers very cautious of how they themselves use categories. For instance, Sacks quotes from two linguists who appear to have no problem in characterising particular (invented) utterances as 'simple', 'complex', 'casual' or 'ceremonial'. For Sacks, such rapid characterisations of data assume 'that we can know that without an analysis of what it is [they] are doing' (1992, 1:429). Forty years on, his comments stand as a criticism of the rapid coding of data that we sometimes find in qualitative research, particularly when researchers analyse interview data.

Back to mundaneity

I will conclude this chapter by returning to my main theme via two more of Chelbin's photographs. The first is of an elderly adult with a little girl. How can we see remarkable things in this mundane encounter?

Note that the caption uses the membership category 'grandfather'. This category keys us in to how we view the photo. If we follow Sacks's suggestion that we try to look for team-like properties between people, this implies that the child on the sofa is not only a grandchild but, in all likelihood, this man's grandchild.

But immediately a number of puzzles come to the surface. What are we to make of the child's bizarre appearance, apparently slumped on a sofa with a vacant expression? Is this any way for a child to behave

Figure 1.3   Grandfather, Russia, 2003

when she is with her grandfather? This is made all the stranger by the fact that she is wearing what looks like a party dress. Even if she is not happy about seeing her relative, shouldn't she be pleased to be dressed up in this way?

Moreover, there is also something strange about the grandfather. Why is his gaze so miserable when grandparents are supposed to derive pleasure from their grandchildren? And why does he stand at some distance from his granddaughter? Aren't meetings with grandchildren supposed to be happy events? If a chimpanzee like Mickey (in the earlier photograph) can put his arm around a child, why can't he have his arm around his own granddaughter?

Looking at Chelbin's photograph gives us no answer to these puzzles – unless we succumb to the impulse to impose some closure on what we see. Instead, its deviation from what we expect asks to ponder the rituals of everyday life.

In a similar way, writers have asked us to look at the contours of mundane existence. Here is Philip Roth on the conclusion of a family funeral:

> That was the end. No special point had been made. Did they all say what they had to say? No, they didn't, and of course they did. Up and down the state that day, there'd been five hundred funerals like

Figure 1.4 Untitled 01

this, routine, ordinary and ... no more or less interesting than the others. But then it's the commonness that's most wrenching, the registering once more of the fact of death that overwhelms everything. (Roth, 2006: 14–5)

Unlike Chelbin or Arbus, Roth takes us straight to the routines of mundane existence without posing puzzles. Nonetheless, he uses his literary vision to bring out what is remarkable about a mundane event. For all three artists, as well as for ethnographers, routines like family funerals are viewable as one of a collection of what Arbus calls 'innumerable, inscrutable habits'.

But, as you may remember, there is another side to this coin. I have been suggesting that extraordinary or remarkable scenes should also remind us of mundane habits. Take another of Chelbin's photographs of circus performers.

In this photo, we see another little girl, this time in a ballet dress. But she balances on a man's hand – an extraordinary scene. Nonetheless, we can retrieve mundane features from this image.

We know that the photograph is taken from Chelbin's work with circus artists. The girl's dress and the man's outfit clearly suggest circus performers. Moreover, we can note the man's proud stare at the camera and the girl's pose with her arms outstretched. Both seem to be asking us to applaud their performance and, unlike the grandfather photo, both seem happy in each other's presence.

So the strangeness of the scene can lead the ethnographer directly into questions about mundane existence. For example, what are the routines of circus life? What kind of relationship between adults and children does it encourage and/or forbid? Such questions lead us in the direction of an ethnography of different work settings.

So circus life involving acrobats and chimps can coexist with mundaneity. The same is true of other apparently extraordinary events such as mental illness. As Alan Bennett comments on his mother's depression and paranoia, 'in all her excursions into unreality, Mam remained the shy, unassuming woman she had always been, none of her fantasies extravagant, her claims, however irrational they might be, always modest. She might be ill, disturbed, mad even, but she still knew her place' (Bennett, 2005: 7).

In my volunteer work with people with dementia living in a residential home, I have, like Bennett, been struck with what they share with us. While these residents (now my friends) may not be able to remember their past lives or even their own names, it would be wrong to assume that they cannot communicate. When they refer to their son as 'my father', we can see this less as a mistake and more as a skill – after all, they have chosen a category from the 'right' collection (i.e. 'family members'). Similarly, even though they may not be able to speak intelligibly, I still have conversations with them. I find that they still recognise basic interactional moves. For instance, when I ask a question, my resident-friends know that an answer is the appropriate next move and produce sounds that serve to do the work of an answer.

When I sing old songs with them, my friends in the home reveal a remarkable ability to remember the words (I am reliant on a songbook!). Even one lady who can no longer speak is still able to show her appreciation of the singing by giving me a 'thumbs up' sign and smiling when I repeat it back to her.

Conclusion

I have noted elsewhere that the philosopher Wittgenstein has important points of contact with what I have been saying. Like Sacks, Chelbin and Arbus, Wittgenstein reminds ethnographers of how hard it is to question situations that appear to be unremarkable. As he writes, 'How hard I find it to see what is *right in front of my eyes*' (Wittgenstein, 1980: 39e).

Unlike the *Guardian* critic who thought it very difficult to write a novel about a single day, in the following passage Wittgenstein asks us to imagine a drama without apparent incident:

> Let us imagine a theatre; the curtain goes up and we see a man alone in a room, walking up and down, lighting a cigarette, sitting down, etc. so that suddenly we are observing a human being from outside in a way that ordinarily we can never observe ourselves; it would be like watching a chapter of biography with our own eyes, surely that would be uncanny and wonderful at the same time. (1980: 12e)

For Wittgenstein, it is wonderful just to observe quite mundane phenomena: 'People who are constantly asking "why" are like tourists who stand in front of a building reading Baedeker and are so busy reading the history of its construction, etc., that they are prevented from *seeing* the building' (1980: 40e).

Wittgenstein reminds us that his kind of philosopher (and our kind of ethnographer) needs both to resist the impulses of contemporary culture and to put on one side conventional academic questions. Causal and historical questions, posed too early, will not help us to understand mundane objects. As Wittgenstein remarks:

> The insidious thing about the causal point of view is that it leads us to say: 'Of course, it had to happen like that'. Whereas we ought to think: it may have happened *like that* – and also in many other ways. (1980: 37e)

Alternatively put: 'God grant the philosopher insight into what lies in front of everyone's eyes' (1980: 63e).

This has been a very sketchy excursion into a very well-known territory. At best, I have tried to offer a few compelling illustrations of what many of us know already.

To repeat a phrase quoted earlier, they underline the fact that good ethnography 'requires a great deal of patience, diligence and caution' (Cowan, 2006: 69).

Ironically, to the extent that university teaches us that great thinkers deal in theories of history or causation, it makes our task harder. Recalling the work of Mass Observation discussed at the beginning of this chapter, a contemporary newspaper sagely observed:

> One fact that has emerged is the difficulty intellectuals seem to have in describing their environment or the daily happenings in their lives.

On the other hand, observation seems to come naturally to people who are living a workaday existence. These take their task seriously and perform it efficiently, perhaps because they recognize the practical value of any attempt to sort out the tangle of modern life. (*Manchester Guardian*, 14 September 1937)

Like 'people who are living a workaday existence', as ethnographers we must learn to take our 'task seriously and perform it efficiently'.

2

On Finding and Manufacturing Qualitative Data

In the previous chapter, I gave you a taste of the way in which qualitative researchers can access fascinating data by observing mundane settings or by finding everyday features in extraordinary settings. I called such an approach 'ethnography'.

However, in order to simplify matters, I have so far glossed over two issues to which we must now turn. First, by no means do all ethnographers display the kind of attention to fine detail that I described. Some desire to tell exciting tales from the field. Others, especially in recent times, displace such detail with what I find to be a depressing concern with highfalutin' theory and experimental writing (see my discussion of postmodernism in Chapter 5).

Second, it bends reality considerably to imply that ethnography is today the main method of qualitative research and that observational material is the main data source. In a way this is hardly surprising given the plethora of materials that invite our attention. These extend beyond what we can observe with our own eyes to what we can hear and see on recordings, what we can read in paper documents and electronically download from the Internet, to what we can derive by asking questions in interviews or by providing various stimuli to focus groups.

However, despite this wide range of material, when it comes to actual research studies, there is hardly an even spread of methods. Nor is it the case that ethnography is just one among many methods. Instead of looking, listening and reading, the majority of contemporary qualitative researchers prefer to select a small group of individuals to interview or to place in focus groups. In this sense, by assembling a specific research sample, linked only by the fact that they have been selected to answer a pre-determined research question, such researchers prefer to 'manufacture' their data rather than to 'find' it in the 'field'. Despite their earnest claims to do something quite different from quantitative research (more 'humanistic', more 'experiential', more 'in-depth'), such manufacture of data to answer a specified research problem is precisely *the* method which quantitative research espouses.

▰▰▰ Four crucial points

I have now raised four further points that demand to be addressed:

- The warrant and good sense of the terms I have been using (e.g. 'manufactured' data).
- The warrant for claiming that 'manufactured' data is in the ascendancy in contemporary qualitative research.
- The 'so what?' question (i.e. if there is such an ascendancy, does it matter?). What kinds of phenomena can you see by using your eyes and ears on the world around you that you might miss by asking questions of interview respondents?
- Since most qualitative researchers are not dopes, how have they looked at the world in such a way as to limit their preferred options in qualitative research design? How might these perspectives provide a kind of mental 'blinkers'?

My first point raises an issue that critical readers may be already asking: what do you mean by 'manufactured data'? Doesn't it assume a dangerous polarity between what is 'natural' and what is 'unnatural' or 'contrived'? As anthropologists like Mary Douglas (1975) have shown us, aren't these precisely the kinds of cultural categories that we need to study in use rather than to impose? Isn't all data 'manufactured' in the sense that 'reality' never speaks for itself but has to be apprehended by means of particular concerns and perspectives and by the simple logistics of research – for instance, where you place your VCR? Moreover, am I implying that there are intrinsically 'good' and 'bad' sources of data? By contrast, as all experienced researchers learn, doesn't your choice of data always depend upon your research problem?

These are indeed important points which will require us to unpack such simplistic terms as 'manufactured' and 'found' data. This is precisely what I intend to do at length later in this chapter once I have offered you some more substance. At the cost of temporarily suspending these points, I will avoid getting bogged down too early in what may look like a game of wearisome definitions.

However, I want to answer the second point straight away. What evidence do I have for my assertion that 'manufactured' data is the pre-eminent concern of contemporary qualitative research?

My first evidence is merely anecdotal. For more than twenty years, I have been advising students who have chosen to do qualitative research projects. During that time, I find that around 90 per cent of my supervisees initially nominate interviews as their preferred data source. Of course, my sample may be skewed but I should point out that, particularly since my retirement from a full-time university post in 1998, it includes students in many different institutions, disciplines and continents.

However, I have less anecdotal evidence. In the 1990s, I did a survey of two social science journals and found that, of the qualitative research articles published in the past 5 years, interviews and focus groups constituted between 55 per cent and 85 per cent of the total. More recently, I analysed the contents of one qualitative research journal between 2008–9. Of the 18 research articles it published, 17 were based on manufactured data (16 interview studies, 1 study based on focus group data).

How might things change in the future? It is possible that the burgeoning growth of the Internet will mean a slight increase in the proportion of published studies based on naturalistic data? Yet, once again, this may be limited by many researchers' preference to interview online participants rather than to analyse what they do on their PCs.

Why not just study the rich seam of naturally-occurring data on the Internet? Why not take advantage of the fact that the Internet now allows us to study past events as they happened through the use of net archives? As Kozinets points out:

> Newsgroups, forums and other bulletin boards, blogs, mailing lists, and most other synchronous media are automatically archived. The Wayback Machine or Internet Archive captures snapshots of the Internet at certain points in time and saves them for future reference. Efficient search engines make accessible every interaction or every posting on a given topic to a specific newsgroup, or every posting by a given individual to any newsgroup. (2010: 72)

Kozinets describes such research as 'netnography' and observes that 'The analysis of existing online community conversations and other Internet discourse combines options that are both naturalistic and unobtrusive – a powerful combination that sets netnography apart from focus groups, depth interviews, surveys, experiments and on-person ethnographies' (2010: 56).

Subject to ethical constraints (Markham, 2011: 122–3; Kozinets, 2010: 137–40, 194–6), by looking at what people are actually doing on the Internet, we might observe the following netnographically related social facts:

- The text of a particular blog posting has been written and was posted.
- A certain social networking group has been formed, and certain accounts have been linked to it.
- A certain photo was uploaded to a particular photo-sharing community, and received 37 comments (Kozinets, 2010:133).

Yet despite the impressive range of social facts available on the Internet and elsewhere, most qualitative researchers still prefer to analyse manufactured data. As Potter and Hepburn observe:

> [S]tandard methods handbooks present interviewing as the default choice for virtually every perspective (phenomenology, ethnography, grounded theory). The situation in sociology is similar. For example, in 2004 the journal *Sociology* published some 56 substantive articles – of these, 20 used interviews or focus groups (often with little justification) and just three used naturalistic data (working with the loosest of criteria). (2007: 277)

My final evidence for this preference derives from my reading of the job adverts for research posts that my daily newspaper, the *Guardian*, provides every Tuesday. Although I can't provide percentages, my impression is that, yet again, in the majority of cases, 'qualitative research' is associated with asking questions of respondents. Let me offer one example which I believe is fairly representative.

In 2003, I came across an advert asking for applications for a research post on a study of 'how psycho-social adversity is related to asthma morbidity and care'. The text of the advert explained that this problem would be studied by means of qualitative interviews. My immediate question was: How can qualitative interviews help to address the topic at hand? The problem is not that people with asthma will be unable to answer questions about their past nor, of course, that they are likely to lie or mislead the interviewer. Rather, like all of us, when faced with an outcome (in this case, a chronic illness), they will document their past in a way which fits it, highlighting certain features and downplaying others. In other words, the interviewer will be inviting a retrospective 'rewriting of history' (Garfinkel, 1967) with an unknown bearing on the causal problem with which this research is concerned.

This is not to deny that valuable material may be gathered from such a qualitative study, but rather that data analysis should address an altogether different issue – narratives of illness in which 'causes' and 'associations' work as rhetorical moves.

By contrast, a quantitative study would seem to be much more appropriate to the research question proposed. Quantitative surveys can be used on much larger samples than qualitative interviews, allowing inferences to be made to wider populations. Moreover, such surveys have standardised, reliable measures to ascertain the 'facts' with which this study is concerned. Indeed, why should a large-scale quantitative study be restricted to surveys or interviews? If I wanted reliable,

generalisable knowledge about the relation between these two variables (psycho-social adversity and asthma morbidity), I would start by
looking at hospital records.

This asthma study seems to have been designed in terms of a very
limited, if common, conception of the division of labour between
qualitative and quantitative research. While the latter concentrates on
data which shows people's behaviour, qualitative research is seen as the
realm where we study in-depth people's experiences through a small
number of relatively unstructured interviews. This led to what I perceive
to be two blunders in the design of qualitative research. First, a failure
to recognise that some research questions might be better studied using
largely quantitative data. Surely the causal question posed here can be
better addressed via a questionnaire administered to a large sample of
asthma patients or by a survey of hospital records to see if there is any
correlation between an asthma diagnosis and referrals to social workers
and/or mental health professionals.

The second blunder is that the research design as stated appears to
misunderstand the wide potential of qualitative research to study such
things as the careers of asthma patients. Why can't qualitative research
study behaviour? For instance, why not conduct an ethnographic study
which observes whether (and, if so, how) doctors in hospitals and primary care facilities elicit histories from their patients relating to psycho-
social problems? Why not study social work and hospital case conferences
to see if such problems are recognised and, if so, what action is
demanded? In short, why assume that qualitative research involves only
researchers asking questions of respondents?

Moreover, the research design elects to present the main research question to respondents themselves. This causes two problems. First, as is well
known in quantitative surveys, if respondents are made aware of your
interests, this can affect their responses. Second, it can lead to lazy
research in which careful data analysis is simply replaced by reporting
back what people have told you.

As Clive Seale has pointed out:

> This is a very common problem in all kinds of studies, but particu-
> larly ones where people mistakenly use a qualitative design to answer
> a question better suited to an experiment or quasi-experimental
> design. People decide, say, that they are going to see if TV violence
> encourages violent behaviour. Instead of doing a survey of what people
> watch on TV and a parallel survey of their tendency to violence, and
> then seeing whether there is a correlation (hoping that there are no
> spurious reasons for such a correlation of course) they just select a

group of people and ask them (more or less) 'do you think TV watching causes violence?'. (Personal correspondence)

Now I want to deal with my third, 'so what?' question. In part, the asthma study already offers an answer: by eliciting 'manufactured' data, we limit considerably the range of phenomena we can discover and may, sometimes, end up pursuing a path better trod by our quantitative colleagues. However, because the 'so what?' question is important, I want to provide some further examples taken from a recent journal article. Since I will shortly point out what I take to be limitations in the approach used, I should emphasise that, in no sense do I take this to be a particularly poor or weak paper – how could I when the paper I have chosen actually cites my work approvingly!

The paper discussed below is taken from the field of organisations and management, but I have some evidence to suggest that the same trends apply in other substantive fields of social science. For instance, my 1990s survey of published articles revealed a similar situation in the study of health and medicine.

The paper, by Alison Linstead and Robyn Thomas (2002) is called: '"What do you want from me?" A poststructuralist feminist reading of middle managers' identities'. Please forget for the moment the theoretical baggage mentioned in the title ('poststructuralist', 'feminist'). The issue of the uses of such theory, if you are interested, is taken up in Chapter 5 of this volume.

Linstead and Thomas state in their abstract that their paper 'explores the process of identity construction of four male and female middle managers within one restructured organisation'. Quite appropriately, they recognise that their sample is small (interviews with just four managers) and shows some recognition of the consequences of their selective use of extracts from these interviews. One such extract from an interview with Wayne is shown in Box 2.1.

Box 2.1   Interview extract

I've changed so much since I started here. A lot of my mates haven't survived the changes ... they were good guys but they weren't in control of what happened to them. I've been lucky, of course I have, but I've worked for it, I've never sat back, I've always tried to get more paper behind me ... you've always got to keep up but it's getting in front that gives you the insurance.

Here is how this extract is interpreted by the researchers:

> [it] rests on a justification that working hard and getting ahead is demanded by both circumstance and by who you are, and being a 'good guy' is not enough as you have to master the situation. Wayne sees this as achieved through qualifications, but these perhaps function as a sign for other activities that he does not mention. He also evinces a degree of paradoxical guilt that he is a survivor, that he is marked out as different from those men he was close to once, although this is precisely what his actions were intended to do. He is genuinely distressed that his friends lost their jobs, but has to remain hardened to this, to keep his sentiments masked, as he knows he could be next. (Linstead and Thomas, 2002:10)

What we have seen of this study raises three sets of questions laid out below:

- What are we to make of the authors' commentary on this interview extract? What does it add to what any reader could make of it? Is it merely the kind of thing that a journalist might add to a report of a celebrity interview? If it is any different from these things, what warrant do Linstead and Thomas have to suggest the significance of what Wayne 'does not mention', to talk about 'paradoxical guilt' and to assert that Wayne is 'genuinely distressed 'but has ... to keep his sentiments masked'? In what sense is this social science analysis or what, perhaps unfairly, is sometimes called 'psychobabble'?
- Like many qualitative interview reports, no stretches of talk are provided which include both the interviewee's answer and the previous, adjacent interviewer's question, request for continuation or display of understanding (e.g. 'mm hmm', 'I see'). As Tim Rapley has pointed out, such an omission fails to recognise that 'interview interactions are inherently spaces in which both speakers are constantly "doing analysis" – both speakers are engaged (and collaborating in) "making meaning" and "producing knowledge"'. (2004: 26–7)
- Research reveals that people invoke multiple identities in both everyday life (Sacks, 1992) and within interviews (Holstein and Gubrium, 1995: 33–4). Why limit research to interviews when you could observe identity construction within the organisation (e.g. by looking at committee meetings and/or employees' files)?

As Clive Seale (personal correspondence) points out, Linstead and Thomas, like many interview researchers, have not treated the interview itself as an observational site, and have ended up 'buying' the respondent's version.

This partly arises because, like the asthma study, this research on middle managers presents the main research question to respondents.

Qualitative researchers' use of the interview as their default method of data gathering is perplexing given what we know about how participants produce their accounts differently for different audiences. As Jonathan Potter and Amanda Hepburn put it:

> Why produce materials that are flooded by social science agendas and researcher categories, where participants work with a range of different interview-related orientations to stake and interest, and where the parties shift between complex research-related footing positions? What is the special magic the interview provides that makes the very complex analytic task of dealing with those endemic and probably inescapable interview features worthwhile? (2007: 280).

Qualitative researchers' almost-Pavlovian tendency to identify research design with interviews has blinkered them to the possible gains of other kinds of data, for it is thoroughly mistaken to assume that the sole topic for qualitative research is 'people'.

Seale has noted how he seeks to contest this common supposition:

> I find that, in order to counteract the tendency towards wanting to do interviews, it helps to repeatedly make the point that many textbooks assume that when one is going to do a research study one always wants to sample 'people' (rather than, say, documents). This helps [students] realise that all kinds of phenomena can be studied for social research purposes (e.g. building design, music lyrics, websites, small ads etc.) and it is then obvious that interviews aren't the only thing to do. (Personal correspondence)

Even when the choice of interviews is thought through (i.e. interviews undoubtedly give you far more rapid results than observation which, when done properly, can take months or years), many research reports offer journalistic 'commentaries' or merely reproduce what respondents say rather than provide detailed data analysis.

Think about how such a detailed analysis might be made of Linstead and Thomas's interview extract. You might begin from the positioning of Wayne's word 'lucky'. Note how it comes immediately after what might be heard as a criticism of his 'mates' who have lost their jobs. Such criticism of colleagues suggests a 'boastful' person who feels 'superior'. The sting of this is removed by invoking 'luck'. Indeed, throughout the extracts provided by Linstead and Thomas, their respondents beautifully attend to and manage how we might hear them by invoking such down-grades immediately after what might be heard as 'boasting' or criticising others. In the next chapter, I examine in greater depth the importance of attending to such a *sequential* positioning of an account.

It is now time to turn to my fourth and final question: Why has this happened? In Chapter 5, I will discuss what I call the 'interview society' – the kind of cultural environment which has made qualitative interviews attractive to researchers. Here I will merely use a very broad brush to touch upon the intellectual currents which underlie this process.

The nineteenth century was the age of romanticism. In both music and literature, the earlier emphasis upon the use of conventional, classical forms was gradually replaced by a focus on the inner world of the artist. So artistic works came to be judged, in part, by how they gave access to the artist's experiences and emotions. This meant that an eighteenth-century's critic's appreciation of a work by Mozart as 'most scientific' no longer made sense. As the next century wore on, although reference might still be made to the formal structure of works, it now became important to refer to both the composer's and audience's emotions as a standard of appreciation. If you have seen *Amadeus* in the cinema or theatre, its focus on Mozart's 'personality' should remind you of the continuing power and appeal of romanticism.

The psychologist Kenneth Gergen points out very clearly what this kind of artistic Romanticism means for how we think about each other: 'The chief contribution of the romanticists to the prevailing concept of the person was their creation of the *deep interior* ... the existence of a repository of capacities or characteristics lying deeply within human consciousness' (1992: 208–9).

Gergen gives us a ready answer to my 'why?' question. It is only a short leap from thinking about the 'deep interior' of the person to favouring 'in-depth' interviews. Indeed, once we assume that people have a 'deep inte-rior', then it is easy to see the contemporary appeal of a whole range of contemporary formats ranging from qualitative interviews to counselling and other 'psy' professions, to TV chatshows and celebrity magazines.

But, you may ask, am I really suggesting that it is an illusion to suggest that nothing lies between our ears? Doesn't this contradict our own 'experience' that we have thoughts and feelings?

My answer to these questions is a bit complicated. No, I do not want to deny that we think and feel. What I would like to contest is the too-ready assumption that what happens between our ears is purely a *private* matter – until accessed by the skills of the research interviewer or counsellor.

Reading other people's minds is certainly not a skill reserved for pro-fessionals. Indeed, as Harvey Sacks points out, we learn about the ability of others to read our minds as children. Sometimes these others are teachers or even, as we may be told, an all-seeing God. Most regularly, however, they are our mothers. For instance, when children are asked what they have been doing, they can find their answer denied by their mother – who wasn't there – 'say[ing] "No you weren't" and the child then corrects itself' (Sacks,1992, 1:115). So schizophrenics who believe that others can read their minds may only be mimicking adult–child talk.

But what about the surely paranoid delusion that other people can *control* your mind? Sacks give the example of somebody saying to you 'Remember that car you had?' Now, even though the car was not on your mind at all, you can't help but remember it. In that sense, the first speaker has indeed controlled your mind. As Sacks puts it, 'people aren't crazy for thinking that other people control their minds. That could not be a source for craziness. That could only be a matter of wisdom' (1992, 2:401).

Sacks wants to show us how, as hearers, we depend upon our ability to read the speaker's mind in order to work out the next action required of us. In this respect, even apparently private matters can be viewed as social and structural.

Take the apparently extreme case of 'memory'. Surely 'memory' is something contained inside our heads and therefore 'private'? In response to such an assumption, Sacks invites us to think about those occasions when we had wanted to make a point but the present speaker had continued or someone else had grabbed the floor. In such circumstances, don't we often 'forget' the topic that we wanted to mention? As Sacks observes, 'if you don't get a chance to say it, when you then get a chance to say it, you've forgotten it' (1992, 2:27). In this respect, memory is not at all private or personal but 'in some perhaps quite dramatic way at the service of the conversation ... It is in some ways an utterance by utterance phenomenon' (1992, 2:27) or, as the novelist Julian Barnes has put it, 'The story of our life is never an autobiography, always a novel ... Our memories are just another artifice' (2000: 13).

But Sacks has still more shocks for romantics. If memory is not simply a private matter, nor is 'experience'. One way to understand this is through Sacks's discussion of storytelling.

Sacks shows us that, when we tell a story (unless we are a bore), we try to find an audience to whom the story will be relevant. Indeed, without such an audience, we may not even remember the story. Storytellers also prefer to display some kind of 'first-hand' involvement in the events they describe. Indeed, people are only entitled to have experiences in regard to events that they have observed and/or which affect them directly. For instance, in telephone calls, events like earthquakes are usually introduced in terms of how you survived. Indeed, such events tend to get discussed less in terms of when they happened but more in relation to when we last talked – our 'conversational time' (Sacks, 1992, 2:564).

In this way, Sacks notes, we seek to turn events into experiences or 'something for us' (1992, 2:563). However, this shows that telling someone about our experiences is not just emptying out the contents of our head but organising a tale told to a proper recipient by an authorised teller. In this sense, experiences are 'carefully regulated sorts of things' (Sacks, 1992, 1:248).

Introducing the notion of 'regulation' into something so apparently personal as 'experience' is just one surprise that Sacks has in store for us. Moreover, for Sacks, in everyday life, we cannot even count on an objective realm of 'facts' to balance apparently subjective 'experience'.

Scientists usually assume that they first observe facts and then seek to explain them. But, in everyday life, we determine what is a 'fact' by first seeing if there is some convincing explanation around. For instance, coroners may not deliver a verdict of suicide unless there is some evidence that the deceased person had a reason to take their own life (Sacks, 1992, 1:123). In that sense, in everyday life, only those 'facts' occur for which there is an explanation (1992, 1:121).

What is the import of Sacks's revelation that, in many senses, what goes on between our ears is a public matter? To me, it suggests that qualitative researchers who unthinkingly prefer to use interviews are barking up the wrong tree. Blinded by a vision of people's 'deep interiors', they remorselessly focus on accessing the insides of people's heads rather than observing how we make 'experiences' and 'motives' publicly available in innumerable everyday contexts.

Sacks once made the telling remark that if his students were really interested in the insides of people's heads, they should become brain surgeons rather than sociologists! In that way, they would discover that, contra romanticism, the only thing that lies between our ears is boring old grey matter.

Indeed, there is something quite curious about researchers providing commentaries on what people say to them in interviews. After all, being a competent member of society means that you can make sense of what strangers tell you without needing a skilled researcher to help you out. To render this situation even stranger, Sacks invents a device that he calls a 'commentator machine'. He tells us that this hypothetical machine might be described by the layman in the following terms:

> It has two parts; one part is engaged in doing some job, and the other part synchronically narrates what the first part does ... For the commonsense perspective the machine might be called a 'commentator machine', its parts 'the doing' and 'the saying' parts. (1963: 5)

For a native-speaking researcher, the 'saying' part of the machine is to be analysed as a good, poor or ironical description of the actual working of the machine (1963: 5–6). However, Sacks points out this sociological explanation trades off two kinds of unexplicated knowledge:

(a) knowing in common with the machine the language it emits and

(b) knowing in some language what the machine is doing. (1963: 6)

But to know 'what the machine is doing' ultimately depends upon a set of pre-scientific, commonsense assumptions based on everyday language and employed to sort 'facts' from 'fancy'. It follows that our ability to 'describe social life', whether as laypeople or sociologists, 'is a happening' which should properly be the 'job of sociology' (1963: 7) to *describe* rather than tacitly to *use*.

I have answered my fourth question by using Sacks's account of a weird commentator machine to show the strange kinds of blinkers that qualitative researchers place over their eyes when they unthinkingly elect to use interviews to answer their research questions. I might also add that this is a circular issue since research questions are often framed by using categories like 'experience' which foreshadow the collection of data by such (mistakenly) 'in-depth' methods.

Sacks's insistence on the priority of describing the everyday 'procedure employed for assembling cases of the class' radically separates his position from contemporary romantic researchers. So when Linstead and Thomas identify 'paradoxical guilt' and 'genuine distress' in Wayne's account of his job, they are working with what Sacks calls 'undescribed categories'. As Sacks puts it, 'To employ an undescribed category is to write descriptions such as appear in children's books. Interspersed with series of words there are pictures of objects' (1963: 7).

For Sacks, most sociologists get by through simply 'pointing' at familiar objects (what philosophers call 'ostensive' definitions). So they are able to give an account of what Sacks's 'commentator machine' is 'doing' by invoking 'what everybody knows' about how things are in society – using what Garfinkel (1967) refers to as the 'etcetera principle' based on treating a few features as indicating the rest to any reasonable person. They thus pretend to offer a 'literal' description of phenomena which conceals their 'neglect [of] some undetermined set of features' (Sacks, 1963: 13).

Such neglect cannot be remedied, as some researchers claim, by assembling panels of judges to see if they see the same thing (e.g. inter-coder agreement as a basis for claiming that Linstead and Thomas's commentary on Wayne's account is reliable). Such agreement offers no solution because it simply raises further questions about the *ability* of members of society to see things in common – presumably by using the 'etcetera principle' as a tacit resource (see Clavarino et al., 1995).

Sacks's problem is how we can build a social science that does better. 'In some way, we must free ourselves from the common-sense perspective' (1963: 10–11) employed in our use of 'undescribed categories'. For Sacks, the solution is to view such categories 'as features of social life which sociology must treat as subject matter' rather than 'as sociological resources' (1963: 16).

What looks like a complicated theoretical solution turns out, however, to involve a quite straightforward direction for research. We must give up defining social phenomena at the outset (like Durkheim's initial definition of 'suicide') or through the accounts that subjects give of their behaviour (Sacks's 'commentator machine'). Instead, we must simply focus on what people *do*. As Sacks puts it, 'whatever humans do can be examined to discover some way they do it, and that way would be describable' (1992, 1:484).

Sacks concedes that this kind of research can seem to be 'enormously laborious' (1992, 1:65). However, he denies critics' claims that it is trivial. You only need to look at the ability of both laypersons and conventional researchers consistently to find recognisable meaning in situations to realise that social order is to be found in even the tiniest activity. The accomplishment of this 'order at all points' (1992, 1:484) thus constitutes the exciting new topic for social research.

Beginning with the observability of 'order at all points', our first task should be to inspect the 'collections of social objects – like "How are you feeling?" – which persons assemble to do their activities. And how they assemble those activities is describable with respect to any one of them they happen to do' (1992, 1:27).

So far, I have been using Sacks's brilliant insights to support my critique of the naive use of interview data. But Sacks also has positive things to say about what we can learn through observation. Some of Sacks's ideas are set out in Box 2.2.

Box 2.2   Sacks on observing everyday life

Take the example of socialising. The ability of some people to be able to enter into conversations with attractive strangers is something that puzzles a lot of us. Indeed, books with titles like HOW TO WIN FRIENDS usually sell very well. What is the knack involved?

(Continued)

(Continued)

Have you ever said 'hello' to a stranger and been rebuffed? The problem is that such a greeting implies that you already knew the person concerned and hence had 'an initial right to use "Hello"' (Sacks, 1992, 1:103). Hence a stranger need not return your greeting.

As Sacks says, one solution to this problem is to begin with questions to a stranger such as:

'Don't I know you from somewhere?'

'Didn't I see you at such-and-such a place?'

'Aren't you so-and-so?' (1992, 1:103)

The advantage of the question form is that it is properly receipted by an answer. So not to answer a question, even if you suspect the motives of the questioner, is a difficult act to bring off. Moreover, having got that answer, the questioner properly may ask *another* question. In that way, conversations get started.

All this means that questions can be an effective 'pickup' device. Indeed, in an exercise where Sacks asked his class to provide examples of utterances which might start conversations with members of the opposite sex, around 90 per cent were questions (1992, 1:49).

Among such questions, routine requests are a particularly powerful pickup device. In addition to the obligation to provide an answer to a question, there is the expectation that we should not be needlessly rude to a stranger making a request for something as mundane as, say, the time. Moreover, the requester knows that (s)he will get a standard, quick response and thus will soon be in a position to ask a further question which may start a longer conversation, for example:

A: When does the plane arrive?

B: 7:15

A: Are you going to San Francisco also? (1992, 1:103).

So questions can be good pickup devices when you happen to find yourself in physical proximity to a stranger. However, things get more complicated when the person you are interested in is part of a larger crowd involved with you in a multi-party conversation. In this situation, Sacks asks, how do people manage to set up a purely two-party conversation?

One possibility is to ask if anyone wants a drink and then to return with the drink to sit next to the particular target of your attention (Sacks, 1992, 2:130). In this way, the right 'territorial' situation can be created. Alternatively, one can try waiting until everybody other than the targeted party has left or, more reliably, if there is music, offer an invitation to dance (1992, 2:131). Indeed, the institution of the dance can be seen as a nice solution to the problem of transforming multi-party into two-party conversation (although the noise of modern clubs may limit this possibility).

I hope you agree with me in finding these examples fascinating. However, you may have another gripe: you may understandably wonder what their relevance is to the 'big' issues out there in society. For all my criticism of Linstead and Thomas's paper, you may say, at least it dealt with important aspects of modern life such as the modern work rat-race. By shifting our gaze from interviews to observation, are we in danger of narrowing our gaze to the minutiae of 'pickups'?

Happily, Sacks shows how a detailed attention to the language we use relates to much wider political issues than how people present themselves. Take the methods used by racists to link particular 'evils' to the work of people with certain identities (e.g. catholics, Jews, blacks, muslims). People don't just simply 'fall' into certain categories, rather we identify people by choosing one of many categories that could be used to describe them. It then follows that

> what's known about that category is known about them, and the fate of each is bound up in the fate of the other ... [so] if a member does something like rape a white woman, commit economic fraud, race on the street, etc., then that thing will be seen as what a member of some applicable category does, not what some named person did. And the rest of them will have to pay for it. (Sacks, 1972: 13)

Not only do Sacks's observations give us a useful hold on how racism works, but they also provide a way of describing one aspect of another 'big' issue – social change. For Sacks, one way we could identify social change would be by noticing 'shifts in the properties of categories used in everyday language and in how these categories were actually applied' (1979: 14). For instance, since 9/11 think how the usage of the category 'muslim' has been transformed.

So Sacks can give us a grip on apparently 'important' issues like racism or social change. However, we have to be careful here because Sacks rejected 'the notion that you could tell right off whether something was important' (1992, 1:28). He uses the case of biology to show how the study of an apparently minor object ('one bacterium') can revolutionise our knowledge. Why assume, for instance, you need to look at states and revolutions, when, as Sacks shows, some apparently tiny object like a question to a stranger 'may give an enormous understanding of the way humans do things and the kinds of objects they use to construct and order their affairs' (1992, 1: 28)?

These extended examples drawn from Sacks's trailblazing lectures forty years ago illustrate what qualitative researchers can learn about the world without needing to interview anybody. They suggest that, all things being equal, we have no need to 'manufacture' data and should prefer to examine what I have called 'found' data.

So far this has been quite a partisan treatment of the debate about how qualitative research should properly be conducted. Indeed, I am sometimes, mistakenly, accused of being 'anti-interview'.

I now want to slow down, as it were, and to go through the debate in a more measured way, taking account of the counter-arguments made by its critics. In doing so, I will replace the somewhat clumsy term 'found data' with the more commonly used description 'naturally occurring data' to denote material that appears to arise without a researcher intervening directly or providing some 'stimulus' to a group of respondents.

The rest of this chapter will consider the answers to a set of questions that arise from the position I have so far taken:

- What are the basic arguments for preferring naturally occurring data?
- What are the limitations of these arguments?
- Is there a way forward which takes on board the (good) arguments of both sides?

Why naturally occurring material is special

This will be quite a short section which will serve to recap what I have been saying up to now by linking Sacks's pioneering work to the arguments of some contemporary researchers. As we have seen, Sacks implied that, when researchers offer commentaries on interviewees' statements, they tend to use commonsense or purely research-driven categories.

Of course, researchers can avoid this problem by simply doing a 'content analysis' which will identify respondents' own categories and count how frequently they use them. Unfortunately, there are two reasons why this is no real solution to the problem that Sacks has raised.

First, when an interviewee uses a particular category (e.g. Wayne's references to 'keeping up' and 'getting in front'), one cannot reliably know whether (and how) he actually uses such a category outside the interview context. What we do know from researchers like Holstein and Gubrium (1995) and Rapley (2004) is that interviewees fashion their categories from researchers' categories (e.g. 'tell me your story') and activities (e.g. 'uh huh').

Second, if categories are utilised in particular contexts rather than simply pouring out of the insides of people's heads, any method we use (even content analysis) cannot transform what interviewees say into anything more than a category used at a particular point in some interview. It follows that if we are interested in institutions rather than interviews, our first thought should be to study those institutions themselves. As Sacks puts it, this means 'attempting to find [categories] in the activities in which they're employed' (1992, 1:27).

Sacks's detailed arguments have largely been ignored by most qualitative researchers, but it is wrong to assume that this means that Sacks (and myself) are completely out on a limb. In particular, some influential contemporary ethnographers contest the conventional assumption, deriving from the early work of Howard Becker, that interviews give us direct access to people's perceptions and that the role of observation is merely to see if such perceptions and meanings are 'distorted' (Becker and Geer, 1960).

Unlike Becker, later ethnographers do not always agree that interviews should play a significant role in field research. For instance, in a book devoted to the writing of ethnographic fieldnotes, we find the following pointed comment:

> [E]thnographers collect material relevant to members' meanings by focusing on ... naturally occurring, situated interaction in which local meanings are created and sustained ... Thus interviewing, especially asking members directly what terms mean to them or what is important or significant to them, is *not* the primary tool for getting at members' meanings. (Emerson et al., 1995: 140)

Sometimes interview researchers will concede Emerson et al.'s point but raise a practical objection. They say that, although interview data can raise the problems of interpretation to which I have been alluding, we often, perforce, must interview simply because we cannot obtain access to the 'naturally occurring situated interaction' to which Emerson et al. refer.

Say you are interested in 'the family'. Surely it will be difficult to obtain access to people's homes in order to understand their family life?

My answer to this question is that the likely unavailability of data which it assumes is actually a giant red herring. In a paper on methodological issues in family studies, Gubrium and Holstein (1987) show how much sociological work assumes that 'family life' is properly depicted in its 'natural' habitat – the home. However, this involves a number of commonsensical assumptions, for example, that families have 'inner' and 'outer' sides (the 'inner' side is located in the household) and that outside of households we obtain only a 'version' of this 'prime reality'.

Conversely, they argue that the 'family' is not a uniform phenomenon, to be found in one setting, but is 'occasioned' and 'contexted'. 'Family' is a way of interpreting, representing and ordering social relations. This means that the family is not private but inextricably linked with public life. So the household does not locate family life. Instead, the 'family' is to be found wherever it is represented.

This means that family studies do not need to be based on either obtaining access to households or interviewing family members. This is because what the 'family' is, is not some stable, unitary object. So, if you are interested in the family, simply study wherever this institution is invoked. If you cannot access a household (or do not want to), try the law courts, probation service, paediatric clinics, newspaper stories and advice columns and so on.

Gubrium and Holstein's alternative direction for family studies closely fits Sacks's approach, while opening up a number of fascinating areas for family studies. Once we conceive of the 'family' in terms of a researchable set of descriptive practices, we are freed from the methodological and ethical nightmare of obtaining access to study families 'as they really are', that is, in their own households.

Issues of household location and privileged access now become redefined as topics rather than troubles – for example, we might study the claims that professionals make for such access. This underlines Gubrium and Holstein's point that family knowledge is never purely private. Even in interviews, family members will themselves appeal to collective representations (like maxims and the depiction of families in soap operas) to explain their own behaviour. Family members also present the 'reality' of family life in different ways to different audiences and in different ways to the same audience.

Of course, Gubrium and Holstein's arguments apply well beyond family studies. They show that, when researching *any* institution, lack of access should not lead us to assume that interviews are the only way forward.

Following Sacks, we can carry this argument even further than either Emerson or Gubrium and Holstein would probably want to go. Take Jonathan Potter's position on this debate. Potter (1996, 2002) has roundly criticised researchers who use his own approach (discourse analysis) for depending too much on interview data and has argued for a greater use of naturally occurring data. Closely following my concept of 'manufactured' data he shows how interviews, experiments, focus groups and survey questionnaires are all 'got up by the researcher'. Instead, he proposes what he humorously calls 'the dead social scientist test'. As he describes it:

> The test is whether the interaction would have taken place in the form that it did had the researcher not been born or if the researcher had got run over on the way to the university that morning. (Potter, 1996: 135)

Potter's test is a useful device for asking questions at the initial stage of research design. However, how far can we take it? Am I (and Potter) saying that interviews and the like are always off-limits to competent qualitative researchers? To answer this question, I must move on to the limits of this extreme position.

Some limitations in the argument: why manufactured data can never be entirely off-limits

I am aware that much of this chapter may so far read as a polemic which seeks to lay down the law about what constitutes 'good' and 'bad' research. I ought to stress, once again, that, consonant with the mandate of this series, what you are reading are merely my own views and there are plenty of good qualitative researchers who part company with some or even all of my argument.

However, even in this context, editorial balance is never a bad thing. So, without withdrawing anything that I wrote earlier, I will now show that there are a number of reasons why we should not take the undoubted appeal of naturally occurring data too far. As I shall argue:

- no data are intrinsically unsatisfactory
- no data are 'untouched by the researcher's hands'
- polarities like naturally occurring data versus manufactured data are rarely helpful if carried too far
- apparently 'good quality' data do not guarantee 'good quality' research
- everything depends upon how you analyse data rather than the data's source.

No data are intrinsically unsatisfactory

This reiterates one of the few principles about which all experienced researchers can agree. There are no 'good' or 'bad' data. In assessing the value of any data source, everything depends on what you want to do with them and on your research question. For instance, as Patrick Brindle has asked (Personal correspondence), how are we to study the social history of past events in living memory without recourse to interviewing?

Such a pragmatic approach to interview data is reinforced by critical comments made by Clive Seale when he read a first draft of this chapter:

> Is it not the case that in medieval times (i.e. before the Romantic movement) when people wanted to find out something (e.g. the people who constructed the Domesday book) they went and asked people for reports? Do we feel that Booth, in his survey of London poverty, was a 'romantic' because he relied on respondents' reports rather than observations? Is it the case that conventional qualitative interviews are always trying to get at the secret inner core of a person, rather than just asking them to report on something they have seen, heard, done etc.? Might it be the case that people think of interviews first for quite pragmatic and commonsense reasons: because this is how anyone tries to find out about experiences they don't know much about: by asking some people who have had those experiences. (Personal correspondence)

Seale's pragmatic approach is illustrated by how Tim Rapley (2004) has chosen to work with interview data. Rapley uses conversation and discourse analysis – a theoretical position deriving from Sacks and Potter. This would appear to rule out using what I have called 'manufactured' data. However, Rapley's topic in his PhD research was precisely how identities get produced in research interviews. Hence not only did he work with interview data, he actually borrowed this data from somebody else's study. Yet this use of (second degree) manufactured data was fully justified by his research topic. Indeed, even Jonathan Potter has recently used (manufactured) focus group data for precisely the same reason (Puchta and Potter, 2004).

No data are 'untouched by the researcher's hands'

As I observed earlier in this chapter, isn't the idea of 'manufactured data' somewhat slippery? Doesn't it assume a dangerous polarity between what is 'natural' and what is 'unnatural' or 'contrived'? Even when we think we are not 'intervening' in the field (e.g. by posing questions to research subjects), our data cannot be entirely 'natural' but will be mediated by the presence of our recording equipment and by the process of obtaining informed consent as required by contemporary ethical standards. Hence isn't it better to refer to 'naturalistic' data since no data is ever untouched by human hands? But, if this is the case, as Susan Speer rightly observes, what happens to the 'dead scientist test' (2002: 516)?

Polarities are usually unhelpful in research

I have called the opposition between 'manufactured' and 'naturally occurring' data a 'polar opposition', that is, it assumes that you have to choose one pole or the other. However, it is usually a good rule of thumb that such polarities work better in the lecture hall than in actual research. Generally speaking, social science should investigate such polarities rather than use them. For instance, as anthropologists like Mary Douglas have shown, we need to investigate how different groups distinguish between what is 'natural' and 'artificial' for them.

'Good quality' data does not guarantee 'good quality' research

Making videos of people engaging in their ordinary activities might appear to be at the other end of the continuum to posing questions to a respondent asked to assume the identity of an interviewee. However, it is dangerous to assume that using the former kind of material guarantees research of high quality. Not only are there always technical issues (which recording equipment you use and where you place it), but your video data will never speak for itself. Instead, you will need to work your way through a number of complicated problems: how will you transcribe and analyse your videos, will you simply use illustrative examples or will you try to be more systematic (and, if so, how)?

Even if you just observe, you will need to find some way of recording your observations. Despite ethnographers' attention to the logic of writing their fieldnotes (see Emerson et al., 1995), most do not confront fully the problematic character of how we describe our observations. Put at its simplest, this relates to what categories we use. As Sacks says:

> Suppose you're an anthropologist or sociologist standing somewhere. You see somebody do some action, and you see it to be some activity. How can you go about formulating who is it that did it, for the purposes of your report? Can you use at least what you might take to be the most conservative formulation – his name? (1992, 1:467)

As Sacks suggests, this apparently trivial problem is actually not resoluble by better technique, like detailed note-taking. Rather it raises basic analytic issues: 'The problem of strategy ... may not be readily handleable by taking the best notes possible at the time and making your decisions afterwards. For one, there is an issue of when it is for the Members that it turns out who did the thing' (1992, 1:468).

In fact, many contemporary ethnographers, now aided by advanced software packages, ignore this problem. In the way Sacks suggests, they simply put in some set of categories derived from lay usage (1992, 1:629). By doing so, of course, we are no wiser of how, in situ, categories are actually deployed and enforced, nor how violations in category use are actually recognised (1992, 1:635–6).

⬤ Everything depends upon how you analyse data

While, in many (but not all) senses there cannot be 'bad' data, there certainly can be flawed data analysis. Such flaws can arise, for instance, where we focus on just one interview extract without analysing its position in a conversation or comparing it to other extracts which might tell a different story. A flaw more relevant to my present argument is when we treat what people say in interviews (or elsewhere) as providing a simple picture of the inside of their heads.

But this need not be the case. Following Sacks, we can treat what people say as an account which positions itself in a particular context (e.g. as somebody responding to an interviewer's question and/or as a person claiming a particular identity, i.e. as a 'family member', 'employee', 'manager' etc.). Here the researcher is viewing what people say as an *activity* awaiting analysis and not as a *picture* awaiting a commentary.

This debate shows that, as Clive Seale has noted, a lot depends on the claims you make about your analysis. For Seale,

> interviews can be treated as a 'resource' rather than a topic as long as researchers are aware of the problem of relying on someone else's report, who often has particular interests in presenting a particular version. If these are taken into account when drawing (cautious) conclusions, then I can't see why one can't do that with interviews too. (Personal correspondence)

If you go further than Seale and treat interview talk as a topic, then both interviews and tapes can be studied as courses of action. Indeed, the distinction between the interview and observation depends on an unexamined separation between 'thinking' and 'doing' (Atkinson and Coffey, 2002: 813).

All this seems to suggest that this has been a worthless debate or, at best, a debate only useful to clear your mind about a dangerous polarity. However, I would not have wasted your time if I believed this was entirely the case. In fact, I think this debate raises a number of issues which are central to the conduct of qualitative research. I will, therefore, conclude this chapter by suggesting a modest way forward.

A way forward

This section unashamedly draws upon a very useful discussion of these issues in the journal *Discourse Studies* (2002) based upon an article by Susan Speer with responses by, among others, Jonathan Potter. Although Speer begins by questioning the polarity between naturally occurring and contrived data and Potter by supporting it, both conclude by conceding that, ultimately, everything turns upon your research topic rather than upon choosing one side of this polarity.

For instance, even though Speer is uncomfortable with the assumption that there is such a thing as 'naturally occurring data', she recognises that research interviews or 'other manufactured' methods of gathering data may not be the best way to research certain topics. So, if you want to study, say, how counselling gets done, why seek retrospective accounts from clients and practitioners or use a laboratory study? Equally, if you are studying gender, she notes that you should be wary of basing your research on interviews where respondents are asked to comment on gender issues. As she observes, you are much more likely to gather reliable data by studying how people actually *do* gender in everyday environments, for example in meetings, email messages and so on (Speer, 2002: 519–20).

Speer also provides a second way to take this debate forward. Instead of making a rigid distinction between manufactured and naturally occurring data, she suggests that we should simply examine how far any research setting is *consequential* for a given research topic.

For instance, in one laboratory study cited by Schegloff (1991: 54), limitations were placed on who could speak. This made the experimental setting consequential for its topic of 'self-repair' and undercut its conclusions. Without such limitations, the study would have been sound.

A second example is a study I reviewed for a journal. Its topic was humour in testicular cancer consultations. The data was derived from interviews with patients. Moreover, there was some evidence that patients had been asked directly about using jokes in their consultations. As I have suggested earlier (and as Speer notes about gender research), such direct questions will influence what people say and are not usually a useful way to investigate a phenomenon.

My final example of how the research setting can impinge on the reliability of data is Drew's (1987) own study of humour. Drew's use of a video-camera might have been consequential if, say, Drew was concerned with the frequency of laughter. However, his focus was on how jokes get done and he argued that the presence of the camera was irrelevant.

In all these cases, the issue, as Schegloff (1991) has put it, is whether the research environment was *procedurally consequential*, that is, whether how the data was gathered influenced its reliability. It demands that researchers attend to and demonstrate that they have thought through the extent to which their findings may simply be an artefact of their chosen method. In this respect a concern to overcome 'procedural consequentiality' is more important than the side of the natural/manufactured polarity upon which your data fall.

Concluding remarks

Through the work of researchers influenced by Sacks, as well as that of linguistically oriented ethnographers, a new programme is starting to assume more importance in qualitative research. Rather than seek to avoid 'bias' through the use of 'neutral' or 'objective' research instruments, this programme treats all research contexts as thoroughly social, interactional occasions (Speer, 2002). Given this position, it follows that the default data source for such researchers are those contexts which societal members ordinarily assemble for themselves. Faced with the ubiquity and complexity of such contexts, why would any researcher seek to create a special research setting in order to study how people behave? To those who argue that some members' practices are difficult to access, we can agree but point out that such unavailability is only apparent and based on commonsense assumptions about where phenomena (e.g. 'the family') are to be found.

Yet, despite these cogent arguments, manufactured research settings, such as interviews and focus groups, have become predominant in qualitative research and even ethnographers usually feel compelled to combine and test their observations by asking questions of informants.

In the light of a recent debate in *Discourse Studies*, I have reassessed the value of the concept of 'naturally occurring' data and its relevance to the programme of qualitative research. Of course, in all research, choice of data must, in part, depend upon our research problem. Equally, there is no question that all polarities should be investigated – particularly where, as here, they involve an appeal to 'nature'.

The moderate tone I have recently introduced should not conceal the strong impulses I derive from my own research experience. This teaches me that, all things being equal, it is usually a good ploy (and certainly an aid to the sluggish imagination) to begin a research project by looking at naturally occurring data. While iron rules are rarely a good idea in research, this rule has worked for me and many of my students. In the next few lines I will explain why I think this is so.

Harvey Sacks continually reminded his students that it turns out our intuitions rarely give us a good guide to how people actually behave. We cannot rely on our memory of what someone said because such memory will not preserve the fine detail of how people organise their conversation. Nor is this problem soluble by using mechanical equipment to record research interviews, for people's own perceptions are an inadequate guide to their behaviour.

By contrast, naturalistic data can serve as a wonderful basis for theorising about things we could never imagine. As Sacks puts it, using what ordinarily happens in the world around us means 'we can start with things that are not currently imaginable, by showing that they happened' (1992, 1:420).

Jonathan Potter has recently extended Sacks's arguments and I can do no better than present below the five virtues that Potter finds in working with naturally occurring data:

- Naturalistic data does not flood the research setting with the researcher's own categories (embedded in questions, probes, stimuli, vignettes and so on).
- It does not put people in the position of disinterested experts on their own and others' practices and thoughts.
- It does not leave the researcher to make a range of more or less problematic inferences from the data collection arena to topic as the topic itself is directly studied.
- It opens up a wide variety of novel issues that are outside the prior expectations embedded in, say, interview questions.
- It is a rich record of people living their lives, pursuing goals, managing institutional tasks and so on. (Adapted from Potter, 2002: 540)

None of Potter's five points deny that interviews or experiments can ever be useful or revealing: 'However, they suggest that the justificatory boot might be better placed on the other foot. The question is not why should we study natural materials, but why should we not?' (Potter, 2002: 540).

3

Instances or Sequences?

In the previous chapter, I considered what kinds of data qualitative researchers should properly gather. However, contrary to the assumptions of many apprentice researchers, collecting data is not even half the battle. Data *analysis* is always the name of the game. Unless you can show that your data analysis is soundly based and thorough, all the effort you put into accessing and collecting your data will have come to naught.

In explaining what 'soundly based' and 'thorough' qualitative data analysis looks like, this chapter offers you a kind of sandwich. The bread consists of a number of relevant research studies. Sandwiched between these is a brief discussion of two great social science thinkers of the last century who showed us why sequences matter.

In quantitative research, numbers talk. With few numbers, qualitative researchers appear to rely on examples or instances to support their analysis. Hence research reports routinely display data extracts which serve as telling instances of some claimed phenomenon. Think back to the interview extract discussed in Chapter 2. Here the use of a thin evidential base rightly provokes the charge of (possible) anecdotalism, that is, choosing just those extracts which support your argument.

One further example of an interview study will make my point. Laura Sheard (2011) was interested in the much discussed topic of female drinking and the dangers to which women were exposed when they went out to drink at night. She interviewed 40 women in the north of England about how they used spaces in the night-time economy and consumed alcohol.

As we saw in Chapter 2, this raises the issue of why one should prefer interview data. Sheard responds in this way:

> Qualitative research places importance on understanding the social world through the perceptions, attitudes and experiences of individuals. In-depth interviews represent one of the best possible ways in which to access the experiences, thoughts and opinions of women on the sensitive topic of personal safety through the medium of a 'conversation with a purpose' ... This method was chosen instead of other qualitative methods such as focus groups or participant observation as it was felt to be the greatest way of 'mining' the richness and depth needed for a topic of this contextual, sensitive and individualistic nature. (2011: 623)

We might note how Sheard identifies qualitative research with individuals' 'perceptions, attitudes and experiences' and consider how this orthodox view neglects social organisation. This is a point I take up at the end of this chapter (see Figures 3.1 to 3.3). More relevant right now is Sheard's version of interviewing as 'mining'. What does mining look like in practice?

We can answer this question by looking at Sheard's report. Here is an extract:

> Being alone and in alcohol-centred spaces was discussed by many women. Some would never go into a pub by themselves, even if they were meeting others. One woman would intentionally arrive 15 minutes late when meeting friends to avoid having to be in a pub or bar by herself. (2011: 624)

Now consider the similarities between what Sheard says here and what a journalist might write about such interviews. In both cases, I suggest, you simply describe what people tell you that bears on the topic in which you are interested. For both journalists and many qualitative interviewers, what people tell you is treated as a (more or less accurate) report on people's perceptions of your topic. And instances of what they say can be offered in support of your interpretation.

Here is one example. Sheard observes that 'A few of the older women interviewed believed their dislike or avoidance of being alone in a pub was related to age and generational differences' (2011: 624). In Extract 3.1 she cites an interview extract in support of her observation.

Extract 3.1   (Sheard, 2011: 624)

Interviewer: Would you ever tend to use spaces like pubs or bars or alcohol-centred spaces?

Participant: I do go out to the pub but only with my husband. I've never been in a pub without somebody with us. I've never walked in on my own. I've never had a reason to. If I was meeting somebody it was always outside and then we would all go in.

Interviewer: Why is that?

Participant: I don't know. Maybe it's my age and thinking that women shouldn't go in the pub by themselves … Like I said I've been in with my husband and my daughter but not on my own. A lot of lasses do now though, don't they? (Marie, 47 years, cleaner)

Like so many qualitative interviewers, Sheard simply restates part of what her interviewee says using the participant's own terms (e.g. 'age') mixed with social science categories (e.g. 'generational differences'). She simply does not attend to the way in which we shape our answers in terms of the question asked and in relation to how the questioner has been identified (in this case, as a researcher).

Indeed, there may be something even more subtle going on in this extract. Notice how the interviewer's first question can be heard as asking for a 'description'. When this answer is finished, she might have asked for another description. But instead she asks 'Why is that?'.

In everyday conversation, unlike courts of law, assessments of insurance claims or classrooms, descriptions often routinely suffice and are not challenged. To ask, as here, 'Why is that?' can thus be heard as a *challenge* to account for your behaviour. And, interestingly enough, her interviewee responds by appealing to her age as a warrant for her account and concluding with something like a proverb ('A lot of lasses do now though, don't they?').

So, by 'mining' her interviews for apposite extracts, Sheard, like so many interviewers, loses sight of how *sequence* is consequential for what we say and do. But, to her credit, in Extract 3.1 she has at least provided her readers with a relatively long extract which includes the interviewer's questions.

Elsewhere, unfortunately, Sheard reverts to simply providing answers without questions and using these answers in a purely illustrative way to support her claims about the data. This is shown in Extract 3.2.

Extract 3.2   (Sheard, 2011: 627)

Sheard's claim

Press coverage and media reports of women being 'drug raped' were at the forefront of the minds of the women interviewed. Significant caution was practised around consumption of alcoholic drinks in order to avoid becoming a victim of drink spiking.

Sheard's evidence

As this woman explains:

I'm very cautious about my drink and where it is and not leaving it and it's the same thing if there are girls in the bar [when she is at work as a bartender], then I will say to them 'Don't leave your

> drinks on that pool table 'cos it takes seconds, doesn't it? You can't
> one hundred percent protect yourself 'cos in the one second that
> you turn your back from the bar and turn back round then some-
> thing could have gone into it. But I think you just have to be very
> aware of who is around you and where your drink is. (Zoe, 22
> years, bar worker)

Although we are given a fairly long extract of Zoe's talk in Extract 3.2,
we simply do not know the question to which Zoe is responding and,
therefore, can only speculate about how she is shaping her answer
accordingly. Moreover, as with Extract 3.1, I would argue that there is a
problem in the information about interviewees provided after each
extract. There are endless ways in which we can describe our identity.
When researchers choose particular identity-characteristics (in these cases
age and occupation), they neglect others (e.g. marital status, number of
friends, siblings etc.). In doing so, they favour particular ways of interpreting what people are saying.

Let me give one, rather different example. In qualitative research, focus
groups, initially only used in consumer and voting studies, are now just
as popular as interviews. Focus groups data are usually gathered by a
moderator offering verbal or visual cues to a small group of people often
chosen to represent a particular sub-group of the population. Unlike a
one-to-one interview, they offer ready access to the views of up to eight
or ten people.

In commercial qualitative research, focus group 'findings' are directly
related to the business goals of the client. This is explained in the comment below by Jonathan Potter, a social scientist who studied commercial
focus groups.

> The companies or organisations who commission the group pay for
> three kinds of output. First, they may have a representative who
> watches the interaction from behind a one-way mirror. Second, they
> will be given a video of the interaction. Third, they will be given a
> report of the interaction written by the moderator (which typically
> summarizes themes and gives sample quotes of people's views).

> Typically, none of these forms of output takes priority over the others.
> This means that the moderator is the central part of the data produc-
> tion. He or she can, for example, display the importance of something
> by drawing attention (e.g. by repeating it) or display its irrelevance to

the business of the group by ignoring it. This will be apparent to the client whether through the one-way mirror or on the video, or in what is quoted in the report. The visibility of the data in market research groups is a much more direct issue than in a social science focus group where considerable sifting and coding may go into the production of a data set for analysis. And there would be no expectation that a research article, say, would include the raw interaction as its data and finding. (Personal communication)

To understand what Potter calls 'sifting and coding' and the study of 'raw interaction', let us look at an example of a social science-based focus group study.

Phil Macnaghten and Greg Myers were interested in how the scientific debate about genetically modified (GM) food was reflected in popular feelings about the subject. Through focus groups, they sought to elicit 'the different ways people relate to animals and … the ways their beliefs and values about animals relate to implicit beliefs about what is natural' (2004: 67).

Extract 3.3 is from their data (please see the Appendix for the transcription symbols used). The extract begins with a leading question from the moderator.

Extract 3.3   (adapted from Macnaghten and Myers, 2004: 75)

(M=moderator; X and Y=participants)

M: Can I just say, so in what ways do you think these animals are natural? (1.0)

X: well, they won't be natural will they=

Y: =they're not natural, they're [man-made aren't they?

M: [they'd be engineered

Y: engineered

For my present purposes, I am only concerned with the issue of how social scientists (as distinct from commercial researchers) might analyse such data. Very helpfully, Macnaghten and Myers discuss two different strategies based, in part, on practical contingencies. Working to a tight timescale, Macnaghten paid more attention to setting up the focus groups than to data analysis. His strategy involved the following three simple steps:

1 Finding 'key passages' quickly (in 200,000 words of transcript).
2 Choosing quotations that made a relevant (and repeated) point briefly and in a striking way.
3 Marking 'quotable themes' with a highlighter (ending up with eight groups of quotes on each of the topics in which he was interested).

The authors note that this simple method offers a rapid way of sorting out data to bear on a particular research topic. When we begin data analysis, we may be in an unknown terrain. In this sense, Macnaghten's method allows us, as they put it, to 'map the woods'.

The kind of rapid answers that can arise through 'mapping the woods' undoubtedly have an appeal to social problem oriented research. However, this method of identifying repeated themes overlooks the fact that the focus group participants are not isolated individuals but are engaged in a conversation. To understand the conversational character of the data, Myers suggests that we need to look at how meaning gets constructed in the interactions between moderator and participants and between the participants themselves. In Extract 3.3 he notes that:

1 X pauses for one second and uses a preface of 'well' which presents his response as unexpected and dispreferred (for a discussion of preference organisation, see Heritage, 1984).
2 Y enters very quickly and M overlaps with him, both of which display preferred actions.
3 Y modifies his term ('manmade') to fit M's term ('engineered'). In this way, Y and M produce a collaborative statement.

This detailed analysis, the authors suggest, is more like 'chopping up trees' than 'mapping the woods'. Unlike the latter approach, it rejects the assumption that there is a one-to-one link between utterances in focus groups and people's 'views' on animals and GM research. Instead, it shows how 'a focus group transcript is a way of recovering, as far as is now possible, a moment-to-moment situation, and the shifting relations of people in that situation' (Macnaghten and Myers, 2004: 75).

However, like any method of data analysis, 'chopping up trees' presents potential problems. First, it is clearly a much slower method than if we proceed by identifying 'key passages'. Second, its linguistic approach may run the risk of losing sight of the research problem with which we began. In this example, critics may justly argue that Myers' sequential analysis has little bearing on the debate about GM food.

Experienced qualitative researchers will recognise that the alternative approaches posed by Macnaghten and Myers exemplify two widely used (and very different) methods for analysing our data. 'Chopping up trees', with its fine-grained sequential analysis, seems a more soundly grounded research method (offering depth) than the scatter-gun approach of simply quoting favourable instances. However, at least 'mapping the woods', whatever its limitations, tells us something about a substantive phenomenon and thus offers breadth.

Later on in this chapter, I will examine another focus group study which, to my mind, successfully combines depth and breadth. However, first we need to see why, in the analysis of qualitative data, sequences matter. To do so, we need to return to those features of our theoretical roots which tend to distinguish what we do from the work of both quantitative social scientists and the kind of commercial research discussed by Potter.

Two thinkers provide the basis for thinking deeply about sequential organisation: the sociologist Harvey Sacks and Ferdinand de Saussure from linguistics. Although these great thinkers were separated by time (Saussure was active in the first two decades of the twentieth century, Sacks in the 1960s and early 1970s) and by their disciplinary background, I will try to show that, in one respect, they offer a common inspiration to reject single instances and to look for sequences. Since Sacks's work will already be familiar to readers of my earlier chapters, I will begin with him and then move on to Saussure.

Sacks on sequential organisation

Saussure and Sacks have a strange feature in common. Both men's work is primarily known through publication of their lectures after their deaths.

Sacks's lectures at the University of California were given during 1964–74. In his very first transcribed lecture, delivered in Fall 1964, Sacks begins with data from his PhD dissertation on telephone conversations collected at an emergency psychiatric hospital. As you read the extracts below, prepare to be puzzled and even bored. You will soon see why they matter.

In Extracts 3.4 and 3.5, A is a member of staff at the hospital and B can either be somebody calling about themselves or calling about somebody else.

Extract 3.4   (Sacks, 1992, 1:3)

A: Hello

B: Hello

Extract 3.5   (Sacks, 1992, 1:3)

A: This is Mr Smith may I help you

B: Yes, this is Mr Brown

Sacks makes two initial observations about these extracts. First, B seems to tailor his utterance to the format provided by A's first turn. So, in Extract 3.4, we get an exchange of 'hellos' and, in Extract 3.5, an exchange of names. Or, as Sacks puts it, we might say that there is a 'procedural rule' where 'a person who speaks first in a telephone conversation can choose their form of address, and ... thereby choose the form of address the other uses' (1992, 1:4).

Sacks's second observation is that each part or turn of the exchange occurs as part of a pair (e.g. Hello–Hello). Each pair of turns may be called a 'unit' in which the first turn constitutes a 'slot' for the second and sets up an expectation about what this slot may properly contain. Given this expectation, A is usually able to extract B's name (as in Extract 3.5) without ever having to ask for it directly. The beauty of this, as Sacks points out, is that it avoids a problem that a direct question might create. For instance, if you ask someone their name, they may properly ask 'Why?' and, in this way, require that you offer a proper warrant for asking (1992, 1:4–5). By contrast, providing a slot for a name cannot be made accountable. So to answer a phone with your name has a function in institutions where obtaining callers' names is important (1992, 1:5–6).

Of course, the fact that something may properly happen once a slot has been created, does not mean that it *will* happen. Take the further example in Extract 3.6 cited by Sacks:

Extract 3.6   (Sacks, 1992, 1:3)

A: This is Mr Smith may I help you

B: I can't hear you

A: This is Mr Smith

B: Smith

Sacks' two procedural rules do not mean that speakers are automatons. What seems to happen in Extract 3.6 is that B's reply 'I can't hear you' means that the slot for the other party to give their name is missed. This does not mean that their name is 'absent' but rather that the place where it might go is closed. As Sacks puts it:

> It is not simply that the caller ignores what they properly ought to do, but something rather more exquisite. That is, they have ways of providing that the place where the return name fits is never opened. (1992, 1:7)

Sacks returns to the issue of 'place' or conversational 'slot' in his Spring 1966 lectures. Slots are places where certain second activities may properly occur after a particular first activity. But how do you demonstrate this? Is 'slot' simply an analyst's category invoked only to explain what the analyst sees?

Sacks answers these questions by showing that members themselves routinely attend to the issue of whether a slot is properly used. One good example of this is the way in which all of us are able to recognise the 'absence' of proper uses of slots. For instance, where someone does not return our 'hello' (and they clearly heard it), we have no problem in seeing that something is absent (1992, 1:308). Indeed, we may properly recount this incident to someone else as an example of a 'snub'.

This example of an 'absent' greeting can be readily seen because returned greetings are part of a category of 'paired objects' which include not only 'greetings' but, for instance, questions-and-answers (1992, 1:308–9). When the first part of such a paired object has been completed, any pause by the second party is seen as *their* pause (i.e. their responsibility). This is because such a first part is hearable as an 'utterance completer' where, once provided, it is the other party's turn to speak and to speak in a way that properly attends to the first part (1992, 1:311).

Such proper attention means that it will be hearably 'odd' if we reply 'hello' to a recognisable question. However, this does not mean we are bound to act in the expected way, nor even that a non-expected reply will always be heard as 'odd'.

As returned greetings show, consecutive activities may be grouped in pairs. This constrains what the next speaker may do but it also constrains the initiator of the first part of the pair. So, for instance, if you want to receive a greeting, you may have to offer one yourself first (Sacks, 1992, 1:673).

Not only greetings but also such adjacent activities as questions-and-answers and summons-and-responses are also paired. This has two consequences. First, the two parts are 'relatively ordered' (1992, 2:521). This means that 'given a first, a second should be done' and what should be done is 'specified by the pair organisation' (1992, 2:191). Second, if the indicated second is not done it will be 'seen to be absent' (1992, 2:191) and a repeat of the first will be offered. For instance, Sacks suggests that quite young children who say 'hi' to someone and then get no reply will usually only go about their business after they have repeated their first 'hi' and obtained a 'hi' in return (1992, 1:98).

The organisation of these kinds of two consecutive utterances provides the concept of 'adjacency pairs' – sequences that are two utterances long and are adjacently placed (greeting–greeting, question–answer, summons–answer). As we have seen, adjacency pairs are 'relatively ordered' because one always goes before the other. They are also 'discriminatively related' in that the first part defines (or discriminates between) appropriate second parts (1992, 2:521).

Adjacency pairs can now be seen as a powerful way of organising a relationship between a current utterance and a prior and a next utterance. Indeed, by constituting a next position which admits only one utterance-type (1992, 2:555), Sacks suggests that 'The adjacency relationship between utterances is the most powerful device for relating utterances' (1992, 2:554).

The power of this device is suggested by two examples relating to the 'summons–answer' adjacency pair. As Cuff and Payne point out, 'the recipient of summons feels impelled to answer' (1979: 151). As they note, one unfortunate consequence of this is that in Northern Ireland during the troubles, when their front doorbell rang and, thereby, constituted a 'summons', 'persons still open the door and get shot – despite their knowledge that such things happen' (1979: 151).

The second example arises in Sacks' discussion of a child's question: 'You know what, Mommy?' (1992, 1:256–7 and 263–4). As Sacks points out, the child's use of 'Mommy' establishes another summons–answer sequence, where a proper answer to the summons is for Mommy to say 'What?'. This allows the child to say what it wanted to at the start, but as an obligation (because questions must produce answers). Consequently, this utterance is a powerful way in which children enter into conversations despite their usually restricted rights to speak.

However, Sacks warns us to avoid the assumption that adjacency pairs, like summons–answer, necessarily work in a mechanical way. For instance, he notes that questions can sometimes be properly followed by further questions, as in Extract 3.7.

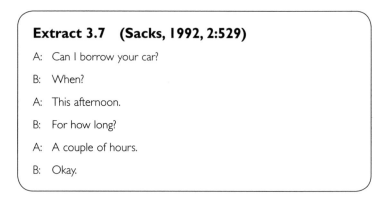

Extract 3.7   (Sacks, 1992, 2:529)

A: Can I borrow your car?

B: When?

A: This afternoon.

B: For how long?

A: A couple of hours.

B: Okay.

In Extract 3.7, B provides the second part of the question–answer pair in line 6, not in line 2. Citing Schegloff (1968), Sacks calls lines 2–5 an 'insertion sequence' (1992, 2:528). Such sequences are permissible in question–answer pairs on the understanding that B will provide the answer when A has finished (1992, 2:529). However, Sacks suggests that, in greetings, unlike other adjacency pairs, insertion sequences are unusual (1992, 2:189).

To summarise what Sacks is saying about how the phenomenon of adjacency works: 'An adjacency pair first part can go *anywhere* in conversation, *except* directly after a first pair part, *unless* the first pair part is the first pair part for an insertion sequence' (1992, 2:534).

Moreover, since adjacency pair first-pair parts can go anywhere, we see, once more, that people have to listen at all times – this time in case they are called upon to do a second-pair part (1992, 2:536). Indeed, we should not assume that adjacency pairs consist of only two utterances.

Not only may there be insertion sequences but, sometimes chains of adjacency pairs may be constructed.

As an instance of such a chain, Sacks notes how we often say things like 'What are you doing tonight?' where our companion knows that an answer like 'Nothing in particular' is pretty certain to lead to a further adjacency pair of 'invitation–response'. In this way, the first question–answer pair serves to 'pre-signal "invitation to come"' (1992, 2:529).

So far my discussion of what Sacks tells us about the organisation of conversation may leave some readers cold. 'Where's the beef?', you may be asking. I now want to show why Sacks is essential reading for any qualitative researcher whether or not they are interested in the niceties of conversations.

Sacks demonstrates the importance of studying sequential organisation by using three striking metaphors:

- economy
- omnipresence
- observability.

I will conclude this section by discussing each briefly.

An economy

Sacks drags us away from our temptation to see conversation as an inner process concerned with the communication of thoughts. This anti-psychologistic thrust is seen in his use of the term 'commentator machine' to describe how interviews work (as discussed in Chapter 2) and of the term 'apparatus' to describe the turn-taking system (see Silverman, 1998: Ch. 4).

Sacks and his colleagues used the metaphor of an 'economy' to describe this apparatus in the following extract: 'For socially organised activities, the presence of "turns" suggests an economy, with turns for something being valued – and with means for allocating them, which affect their relative distribution, as in economies' (Sacks et al., 1974: 696).

This concept of 'an economy' powerfully directs us away from our temptation to treat talk as a trivial outpouring of our individual experiences. Instead, like goods and services, turns-at-talk depend on a system for their distribution. Moreover, such turns have a value, seen in the potential 'profits' of obtaining the floor and potential 'losses' (e.g. of memory) in failing to get a turn at a particular point. In this way, the metaphor of 'economy' reminds us of the power and factual status of a turn-taking system which incorporates gestures and movements as well as talk (think, for instance of how we understand auctioneers' movements as they look round the saleroom and as they bang their gavels on their desks; see Heath and Luff, 2007).

⬤ Omnipresence

This power is reflected in the way in which speakers attend to the conversational rules we have discussed in all social contexts. Even the apparent boundaries of different cultures seem to matter little in this regard.

We see this in a joint paper that Sacks wrote with the anthropologist, Michael Moerman. Moerman and Sacks (1971) note basic similarities between Thai and American English speakers. In Thai, just as much as in American English, one speaker talks at a time with no gaps or overlaps. Equally, in both 'cultures', this is accomplished by speakers noticing and correcting violations, collaboratively locating transition points, collaboratively locating next speaker and listening for completions, turn transitions, insults and so on.

As these authors put it, in both Thai and American English

> participants must continually, there and then – without recourse to follow-up tests, mutual examination of memoirs, surprise quizzes and other ways of checking on understanding – demonstrate to one another that they understood or failed to understand the talk they are party to. (Moerman and Sacks, 1971: 10)

As in Sacks's lectures, these authors remind us that we should not be surprised about how quickly people can do all these things: 'The instant availability of elaborate rules of grammar shows that our naive notion of how little the human brain can do quickly is wrong' (Moerman and Sacks, 1971: 11).

However, this 'instant availability' and omnipresence should not be taken to mean that conversational rules are coercive. Instead, as Sacks notes below, such rules achieve their relevance by being attended to and used:

> Somebody once said to me that they found people who violated the A-B-A-B rules, as if that ought to be something enormously shocking ... That is, as if, in fact, A-B-A-B would characterize any two-party conversation as a natural law, rather than it was something that persons attended to and used in various ways, and something that could tell people that, and *when*, it's their turn to speak. (1992, 1:524)

▬▬ Observability

Despite Sacks's appeal to mechanical idioms, there is nothing abstract or purely theoretical in what Sacks is saying. Sacks sought to give us a way of accessing people's observable activities rather than trying to build a self-enclosed system of rules and categories. This means that the 'orderliness' he describes below is an orderliness which ordinary people rely upon and use:

> [I]nsofar as the materials we worked with exhibited orderliness, they did so not only to us, indeed not in the first place for us, but for the co-participants who had produced them. (Schegloff and Sacks, 1974: 234)

The upshot of this is that 'problems' have to be observable problems for members in order to be interesting for analysts (1974: 234). But the 'ready observability' to which Sacks refers below implies something deep and profound:

> [O]mnipresence and ready observability need not imply *banality*, and, therefore, silence. Nor should they only set off a search for exceptions or variation. Rather, we need to see that with some such mundane occurrences we are picking up things which are *so overwhelmingly true* that if we are to understand that sector of the world, they are something we will have to come to terms with. (Sacks, 1987: 56, my emphasis)

'Coming to terms with' this omnipresence gives us our research task. For Schegloff and Sacks, we must seek to achieve nothing less than 'a naturalistic observational discipline that could deal with the details of social action(s) rigorously, empirically and formally' (1974: 233).

Harvey Sacks was the pre-eminent modern thinker who instructs us to deal in sequences. However, Sacks is often seen as the founder of an approach ('conversation analysis' or CA) which some qualitative researchers view, quite wrongly, as sectarian or irrelevant to their concerns.

I now want to show that the relevance of sequential organisation extends far beyond those who use CA. To achieve that end, I will refer, as promised, to an earlier founding figure in social science – Ferdinand de Saussure. Following that path, I will suggest that Saussure's focus on the articulation of different elements lays the basis for research based on sequences rather than instances.

▬▬▬ Saussure on sequential organisation

Saussure (1974) asks us to study the ways in which relationships and differences are articulated within sign systems such as traffic lights. He rejects a substantive view of language – concerned with the correspondence between individual words and their meanings – in favour of a *relational* view, stressing the system of relations between words as the source of meaning. According to this view, signs are not autonomous entities but derive their meaning only from the place within a sign system. What constitutes a linguistic sign is only its difference from other signs (so the colour red is only something which is not green, blue, orange etc.). For instance, the status of any train arises from its place in a timetable. So, if the 10.30 from Zurich to Geneva does not leave at 11.00 it is still the 10.30 train.

Signs can be put together through two main paths. First, there are combinationary possibilities (for example, the order of a religious service or the prefixes and suffixes that can be attached to a noun – e.g. 'friend' can become 'boyfriend', 'friendship', 'friendly' etc.). Saussure calls these patterns of combinations 'syntagmatic relations'. Second, there are contrastive properties (e.g. choosing one hymn rather than another in a church service; saying 'yes' or 'no'). Here the choice of one term necessarily excludes the other. Saussure calls these mutually-exclusive relations 'paradigmatic oppositions'. As in the railway timetable, signs derive their meaning only from their relations with and differences from other signs.

Saussure's argument seems mainly to have been taken to heart in the analysis of textual or visual data – perhaps because such data is almost self-evidently articulated. However, there are more widely applicable gains for data analysis in Saussure's approach. Once we recognise that 'no meaning resides in a single element', we need to think twice about searching data for individual instances or examples. In interpreting any instance, we cannot neglect the sequence in which it is embedded. So, for instance, analysis based on a single answer by interviewees will usually be inadequate. Thorough analysis must usually be based on an extended sequence of interviewer–interviewee talk (see Rapley, 2004).

However, this example pushes Saussure much further than he was prepared to go.

Saussure's concern for articulation is always at the level of structures and systems rather than interaction ('*langue*' not '*parole*'). Yet articulation occurs not only at the level of impersonal systems. As we shall see in the data extracts that follow, participants are themselves deeply attendant to relations between different activities. This is shown, for example, in the complex ways we have of delivering and receiving invitations. So, following an invitation, the inviter may treat a pause as indicating some problem and provide an 'excuse' (e.g. 'or perhaps you are too busy right now') (see Heritage, 1984: 241–4).

Given that we all demonstrably work with and upon sequences of actions, this means that syntagmatic relations are much more local than Saussure was prepared to acknowledge. In the examples that follow, I will show how data analysis can pay close attention to the local embeddedness of interaction while drawing inspiration from Saussure's emphasis on the articulation of the relation between elements. Although Saussure is most cited in linguistics and structural anthropology, he provides a simple rule that applies to us all. In a rebuke to our reliance on instances, Saussure tells us that 'no meaning exists in a single item'. Everything depends upon how single items (elements) are articulated.

One everyday activity in which the social world is articulated is through the construction of sequences. Just as participants attend to the sequential placing of interactional 'events', so should social scientists. Using examples drawn from focus groups, fieldnotes and audiotapes, I argue that the identification of such sequences rather than the citing of instances should constitute a prime test for the adequacy of any claim about qualitative data.

My earlier discussion of Macnaghten and Myers's (2004) work on attitudes towards GM food raised issues about form versus substance. Can a concern with articulation and sequential organisation tell us about more than conversational structures? To obtain an initial answer to this question, I will discuss a second focus group study in which such substantive matters are more clearly highlighted.

Positive thinking

Sue Wilkinson and Celia Kitzinger (2000) were interested in the way in which both laypeople and many medical staff assume that 'positive thinking' helps you cope better with cancer. They point out that most of the evidence for this belief derives from questionnaires in which people tick a box or circle a number.

By contrast, Wilkinson and Kitzinger prefer to treat statements about 'thinking positive' as actions and to understand their functions in particular sequences of talk. Put simply, they seek to insert 'scare marks' around positive thinking and to examine when and how it is used.

Let us look at one data, shown in Extract 3.8, that they use from a focus group of women with breast cancer.

Extract 3.8   (Wilkinson and Kitzinger, 2000: 807)

Hetty: When I first found out I had cancer, I said to myself, I said right, it's not gonna get me. And that was it. I mean (*Yvonne:* Yeah) obviously you're devastated because it's a dreadful thing

Yvonne: [*overlaps*] yeah, but you've got to have a positive attitude thing, I do

Betty: [*overlaps*] but then, I was talking to Dr Purcott and he said to me the most helpful thing that *any*body can have with *any* type of cancer is a positive attitude

Yvonne: a positive outlook, yes

Betty: because if you decide to fight it, then the rest of your body will st-, will start

Yvonne: motivate itself, yeah

Betty: to fight it

In this extract, Hetty's account of feeling 'devastated' by a cancer diagnosis is met by appeals to a 'positive attitude' by both Yvonne and Betty. On the surface, then, Extract 3.8 seems to support the idea that positive thinking is an internal, cognitive state of people with cancer. However,

> this overlooks the extent to which these women are discussing 'thinking positive' not as a natural reaction to having cancer (the natural reaction [mentioned by Hetty] is that, 'obviously you're devastated because it's a dreadful thing'), but rather as a moral imperative: 'you've got to have a positive attitude'. (Wilkinson and Kitzinger, 2000: 806–7)

So Wilkinson and Kitzinger's analysis suggests two different ways in which these women formulate their situation:

- Positive thinking is presented as a moral imperative, part of a moral order in which they should be thinking positive.
- Other reactions (including fear and crying) are simply described as what 'I did' not as 'what you have got to do'.

This distinction shows the value of looking at how talk is organised and not just treating it 'as providing a transparent "window" on underlying cognitive processes' (Wilkinson and Kitzinger, 2000: 809). By contrast, Wilkinson and Kitzinger's focus on sequences of talk allows us to get a quite different, more processual, grasp of the phenomenon.

Moreover, in this version of 'chopping up trees', we do not lose sight of the substantive phenomenon. Unlike questionnaire studies, which usually simply confirm lay or medical beliefs about the usefulness of certain mental responses to life-threatening illness, this research reveals that expressions of positive thinking may have more to do with public displays of one's moral position than with how people actually respond to their illness.

Such a conclusion provides new insights of potentially great value to both patients and healthworkers – issues of the applicability of good qualitative research discussed in my next chapter. At this stage, it is worth reflecting that Wilkinson and Kitzinger's findings are simply not available from answers to questionnaires or, more relevantly, from conventional qualitative analysis of the data which, no doubt, would find multiple instances of positive thinking within these women's talk.

Wilkinson and Kitzinger show how close analysis of sequential organisation can be practically relevant. Extracts 3.9 and 3.10, drawn from my own tape-recorded data, seek to underline this point.

Analysing audiotapes of HIV-Test counselling

John McLeod has reminded us that 'almost all counselling and psychotherapy research has been carried out from the discipline of psychology' (1994: 190). Given the dominance of experimental and/or statistical methods favoured in psychology, one consequence has been a focus on quantitative studies which apply outcome measures to individuals.

Psychological issues have also been to the fore in interview studies. Although these have sometimes been based upon open-ended questions and qualitative data analysis, the main concern has been to elicit changes in perception and knowledge. This focus upon individuals has meant that what people say has been treated as a more or less transparent window on their world(s).

In designing my research on HIV-test counselling, I used a two-prong strategy to provide a different view of the phenomenon. First, instead of using measures of outcome, I chose to study how HIV counselling worked in actual counsellor–client interviews. Second, rather than look at the client in isolation, I examined sequences of counsellor–client talk (see Silverman, 1997 and, for a shorter version, Silverman, 2011: 61).

At all the HIV-testing centres I studied, counsellors tried not to make assumptions about why people had come for an HIV-test. So pre-test counselling usually began with a question about why the client was there. Extract 3.9 starts in just this way. It is at the very beginning of a counselling session held at the sexually-transmitted disease department of a hospital in a provincial British city. When asked by the counsellor (C) about why he wants an HIV-test, this male patient (P) tells a story about what happened on his girlfriend's holiday.

Extract 3.9   (adapted from Silverman, 1997: 78)

1C: could you tell us why you've come for an HIV test today=

2P: =well basically because I'm worried that I might have AIDS (0.2) er (0.2) when my girlfriend was on holiday in (.) [X] in April with her friend

3C: mm hm

4P: I didn't go because I was busy … she came back (0.6) er April … and it's now November she's just told me that she had sex with a [Xian] when she was there well not actually had sex but this she said that this guy (0.2) this is what she told me this guy had (.) forced herself (.) hisself upon her you know (0.6) er::

       [*further details*]

5P: so: that's what I'm worried about (0.8)

6C: [mm

7P: [and it's been unprotected sex as well

As you read P's account, notice how he displays massive attention to the way his story of his girlfriend's holiday will be heard. 'With her friend' (turn 2) tells us that his 'girlfriend' had not gone away on her own, where going away on your own *may* be heard as implying a problem with a relationship. 'Her friend' does not tell us the gender of the 'friend'. However we know that, if that gender had been male, it would have massive implications for the story that is being told and, therefore, P would have been obliged to tell us. Given that he doesn't, we must assume that 'her friend' is 'female'. Moreover, we can also assume, for the same reason, that it is not a sexual relationship.

But P also leaves a question hanging about why he had not accompanied his girlfriend given that 'going on holiday together' can be heard as appropriate to the girlfriend/boyfriend relationship. 'I didn't go because I was busy' (turn 4) attends to this question. He shows that this 'not going' is accountable and provides its warrant: 'because I was busy'. P makes accountable that he did not accompany his girlfriend on her holiday, thereby invoking the *routine* character of described events and, thereby, constituting his described behaviour as morally acceptable 'business as usual'.

P's account also provides a description of an event that may be heard in terms of other moral issues. 'She was on holiday' (turn 2) conjures up the category 'holidaymaker', which can be heard to imply innocent enjoyment but may also be associated with other activities (e.g. holiday 'romances', holiday 'flings'). Because we know that holidays may be a time when moral inhibitions may be temporarily lifted, the upcoming description of potentially 'promiscuous' behaviour is potentially downgraded or at least made comprehensible.

She's just told me (.) that she had sex with (.) a [Xian] when she was out there' (turn 4) consists of a series of highly implicative descriptions of activities. Having 'sex' with a third party implies 'being unfaithful'. Although the earlier description 'on holiday' (confirmed by the place-locater 'when she was out there') may make this description understandable, it may not make it excusable. As we shall see, P engages in considerable interpretive work to preserve the moral status of his girlfriend in a way that does not threaten his own status as a 'reasonable' person.

'Well not actually had sex with' (turn 4): here the damaging description 'having sex [with a third party]' is immediately repaired by B. Thus we have to suspend the implied category 'unfaithful girlfriend'. But this repaired description is ambiguous. For instance, are we to hear 'not actually sex' as a physical or social description of the activity?

'She said that this guy (0.2) this is what she told me this guy had (.) forced herself (.) hisself upon her you know' (turn 4). It is clear from his next utterance that P is attending to this ambiguity as something in need of further explication. If 'he forced ... hisself upon her', then we are given a description which implies the categories rapist/victim where 'victim' implies the activity of not giving consent.

So P reworks his original category 'having sex', with its damaging implications, by positing the absence of consent and thus a withdrawal of the warrant of the charge 'unfaithful girlfriend' and a return to a description of the events without any charge.

However, there is a further nice feature embedded in P's description. It arises in its preface: 'she said that this guy (0.2) this is what she told me'. P's story of these events is thus doubly embedded (both in 'she said' and in 'this is what she told me'). How does 'this is what she told me' serve to repair 'she said'?

We can unpick the nature of this repair by recognising that, when somebody offers an account, the upshot of which puts them in an unfavourable light, we may suspect that they have organised their description in order to put themselves in a more favourable light. So, if P had simply reported what his 'girlfriend' had said about this incident, then, although he would be implying that he was a 'trusting partner', he could be seen as 'too trusting' (i.e. as a dope).

Now we see that 'this is what she told me' makes him into an astute witness by drawing attention to the potential credibility problem about his girlfriend's account. However, note that, unlike this comment, P is *not* directly stating that his girlfriend is to be disbelieved. Rather her story is offered just as that – as her *story* without implying that P knows it to be true or false.

The beauty of P's repair into 'this is what she told me' is that it puts him in a favourable light (as an astute observer), while not making a direct charge against his girlfriend's veracity (an activity which would allow us to see him as a 'disloyal partner'). This allows a hearer of his story to believe or disbelieve his girlfriend's account and permits him to go along with either conclusion.

Is this the story of an unfaithful girlfriend or of someone who has been shamefully assaulted? However, we decide, P fits himself into the descriptor 'loyal partner' and so is in the clear. P's elegantly crafted story leaves it up to the hearer to decide which story best describes these 'events'.

Extract 3.10 continues on from the previous extract, and shows how C chooses to hear P's account.

Extract 3.10   (adapted from Silverman, 1997: 78)

8 C: right: so obviously someone had forced (0.2) himself on her=

9 P: =yeah=

10C: =hh there was: nothing she could do

11P: mm hm but apparently that's what they're like out there: you know

---

C elects to ignore the ambiguities brilliantly embedded in P's story. Note how her account of the upshot of what she has just heard is prefaced by

'so obviously' (turn 8). But her response is not simple-minded. By elect-
ing to hear this as a story of a rape (rather than an instance of promiscu-
ity), C is attending to the nature of her task which is, after all, to do with
her client's perception of risk rather than the moral status of his sexual
partner.

Notice how P speedily (turn 9) agrees with C's choice of one version of
'what happened', even underlining and explaining C's version (turn 11).
Having set up his story as ambiguous, P would put himself in a difficult
situation if he did not follow how C hears it. To persist in an explanation
which has so obviously been rejected by C (his girlfriend's possible prom-
iscuity), P might now define himself as a disloyal partner.

Through C's response, P discovers what he meant all along (his girlfriend was raped). This reminds us that sequential organisation is not just
an abstract matter dealt with by obscure social scientists but is, rather,
something attended to in great detail by societal members. Members are
deeply and skilfully involved in analysis of the upshot of their own and
other's actions.

So far, so good. But what is the practical relevance of all this? First,
such attempts to understand the skills of the parties involved, as displayed in situ, provide a much more adequate basis for training practitioners than normative instruction or even role-plays (see Silverman,
1997). Second, it makes us realise that supposedly reliable measures of
'outcome' look problematic once we see that what 'really happened' is a
puzzle upon which participants themselves work in real time.

My final two examples, drawn from audiotapes and fieldnotes, focus
upon this feature even more directly, showing how the question 'really?'
may be used as a charge against the truthfulness of a participant's account.

Two cleft-palate clinics

These clinics treat children born with hare lips and/or cleft palates. Cleft-
palates can stop babies feeding and so are usually repaired in the first few
months of life. A hare lip is treatable by routine, low-risk, cosmetic surgery usually carried out when the patient is in their teens. The rationale
for delaying cosmetic surgery in the cleft-palate clinic is that, since
appearance is a matter of personal judgment, it is best left until somebody is of an age when they can decide for themselves rather than be
influenced by the surgeon or their parents. In practice, this reasonable
assumption meant that the doctor (D) would ask the young person concerned a question in the format shown in turn 1 of Extract 3.11, taken
from an English clinic.

Extract 3.11   (Silverman, 1987: 165)

D: What do you think about your looks Barry?

(3.0)

B: I don't know

D: You heh heh doesn't worry you a lot.

Barry's answer was common at this clinic. Short of a later self-correction or a persuasive parental intervention (both difficult to engineer), it meant that many such patients did not get cosmetic surgery.

Drawing upon evidence of this kind, I argued that questioning such young people about their looks set up the consultation as a psychological interrogation likely to lead to non-intervention. This was strengthened by the fact that, later in the consultation, it became clear that Barry (who is twelve), after all, did want cosmetic surgery. Barry's case and that of others showed that these adolescent patients had far less difficulty when they were simply asked whether they wanted an operation rather than being asked to assess how they felt about their appearance. So here we can immediately see a practical outcome from such detailed 'chopping up trees'. However, a visit to a clinic in Brisbane, Australia, provided me with the deviant case shown in Extract 3.12.

Extract 3.12   (Silverman, 1987: 182)

D: Do you worry at all about your appearance?

S: Oh I really notice it but I um if it could be improved, I'd like to get it done. I really worry about it.

In one leap, Simon (S) seems to have overcome the communication difficulties that a question about your appearance usually generates in these clinics. He freely admits that he 'notices' and 'worries' about his looks and, consequently, would 'like to get it done'. What are we to make of this apparently deviant case?

The first thing to report is that, at 18 years of age, Simon is considerably older than Barry and the other children seen in my English clinic. So reticence to discuss one's appearance may be age related and different medical strategies may be applied to different age groups.

However, there was something more interesting about Simon's case. Extract 3.13 (a continuation of Extract 3.12) shows how his reports about his worries were treated by doctors in his clinic.

Extract 3.13   (Silverman, 1987: 183)

S: I really worry about it.

D: *Really?*

S: Yes.

D: Not really but *really?*

S: But *really* yes.

What is going on in Extract 3.13? Why is Simon's apparently straightforward response subject to further questioning? To answer these questions, I noted comments made by a doctor before Simon had entered the room. These are shown in Extract 3.14.

Extract 3.14   (Silverman, 1987: 180)

D: He's er (0.5) it's a matter of deciding whether he should have an operation. And, er, what we are concerned about is his degree of maturity which it will be very interesting for you [*D turns towards me*] to make a judgment on when he comes in.

We see from this extract that, even before Simon enters the room, his 'degree of maturity' will be an issue. We are advised that Simon's answers should not stand alone as an expression of his wishes but should be judged as mature or immature and, perhaps, discarded or reinterpreted.

After Simon leaves, this doctor worries some more about what Simon's answers 'really' mean (see Extract 3.15).

Extract 3.15   (Silverman, 1987: 186)

D: It's very difficult to assess isn't it? Because he's pretty sophisticated
      in some of his comments and it's er (1.0) it's just the, you know,
      continuously sunny nature that's troubling me a little bit about the
      problem as to whether it should be done.

Eventually, this doctor concludes that Simon's relaxed manner is merely 'a cover-up' for his self-consciousness about his appearance. Although this is rather an odd conclusion since Simon has freely admitted that he is concerned about his appearance, it generates general consent and all the doctors present agree that Simon is 'motivated' and should have his operation.

This deviant case considerably added to my understanding of the mechanics of decision making in the cleft-palate clinic. The English data had suggested that asking young people about their appearance tended to set them problems which could lead away from the cosmetic surgery they might want. The Australian data showed that, even where a patient confidently reported his concern about his appearance, this created a further complication. In this case, the doctors worried about how someone so concerned could present themselves in such a confident (or 'sunny') manner.

A Catch-22 situation was now revealed. The doctor's practical reasoning unintentionally resulted in the following impasse:

1   To get surgery, you needed to complain about your appearance.
2   Those who were most troubled about their appearance would often be the least able to complain, so they would not get surgery.
3   Patients who did complain would be viewed as self-confident, hence their underlying troubles were open to doubt and they too might not get surgery.

The impasse derived from the coupling of the doctors' understandable desire to elicit their patients' own views with psychological versions of the meaning of what their patients actually said. This underlines the importance of understanding the versions that participants actually employ in their interactions and avoiding the search for a stable mental state 'behind' someone's talk.

Once again, by locating single utterances within a sequence of talk, we are able to see the process through which they take on meaning. It remains to explore how far this process is purely interactional. To do this, I will take one further case which, although it is from a very different setting, seems to be very similar to what we have seen in the Australian cleft-palate clinic.

 'Really?'

Around the time I was observing the cleft-palate clinics, Gubrium (1988) was doing an ethnographic study of Cedarview, an American residential treatment centre for emotionally disturbed children. Extract 3.16 involves three boys (aged 9–10) who are talking in their dormitory. Gubrium reports that he overheard this conversation from an adjacent room while reading comics with other boys.

Extract 3.16 (Gubrium, 1988: 10)

Gary:	can you really get firecrackers from your brother?
Tom:	really!
	[Gary produces 'a chain of accusatory exchanges' that play on the word 'really']
	[Gary and Bill press Tom to tell the truth 'or else' asking Tom whether he was just kidding]
Tom:	really, really, really.
Gary and Bill:	[jostling Tom] no you didn't … you're lying.

In this extract, Gary and Bill are challenging Tom about his access to firecrackers. Compare what is said to what we have just seen in the Australian cleft-palate clinic (Extract 3.17).

Extract 3.17 (Extract 3.13 repeated)

S:	I really worry about it.
D:	Really?

(Continued)

> *(Continued)*
>
> S: Yes.
>
> D: Not really but *really*?
>
> S: But *really* yes.

Despite two very different settings and participants (a peer group and a professional–client interview), note how participants systematically search for what 'really' is the case, using that term to frame questions and to provide answers. In formal terms, both extracts look like the kind of charge–rebuttal sequences that are common in courts of law. Is it appropriate to say that we are dealing with a single phenomenon which happens to be located in a variety of contexts?

Yes and no. An analysis of the features of charge–rebuttal sequences is indeed a useful exercise since it can identify the various strategies available to people to make or rebut charges. However, we must not exclude the different agendas the participants bring to different contexts and the resources they can draw upon in, say, medical clinics, peer-group interaction and law-courts. Without this further step, our analysis runs the danger of becoming purely formalistic and, thereby, likely to lack the kind of practical relevance in which I am interested.

Gubrium (1988) suggests how we can reframe this argument to mark out the limits of two different kinds of ethnography. *Structural ethnography* simply aims to understand participants' subjective meanings. It makes great use of open-ended interviews and, as such, is the most common approach. By contrast, *articulative ethnography* seeks to locate the formal structures of interaction. It is usually based on audio- or videotapes of naturally occurring interaction and identifies sequential structures like charge–rebuttal sequences or preference organisation. Gubrium argues that, although both these kinds of ethnography answer important questions, they cannot, even in combination, define the whole of the ethnographic enterprise. To do this, we need to understand the context in which the parties generate their meanings and interactions.

To meet this goal, *practical ethnography* recognises that members' interpretations are neither limitless nor purely formal. For example, in Gubrium's residential home, staff members would construct particular versions of children in different contexts, for example, a treatment review team versus a meeting with the child's family. Again, charge–rebuttal sequences may look very different in children's talk versus a clinic or

1 **Structural ethnography:** the organisation and distribution of subjective meanings within a community (e.g. friendships and alliances among children; how staff members responded to the firecracker episode with different versions of Tom's personality – 'a chronic liar', 'a keen bargainer'), i.e. the WHATS of social life (mapping the woods).

2 **Articulative ethnography:** how meanings are locally constructed, i.e. the HOWS of interaction (e.g. local organization of accusation–defence sequences in Extracts 4 and 5 (chopping up trees).

3 **Practical ethnography:** 'practitioners of everyday life not only interpret their worlds but do so under discernible auspices with recognizable agendas' (Gubrium, 1988: 34), for example, accusation sequences look different in children's talk versus a clinic or courtroom.

Figure 3.1   Gubrium's three kinds of ethnography

courtroom. Such actions are, as Gubrium (1988) puts it, 'organisationally embedded', that is, different settings may provide the participants with differing meanings and interactional resources. Gubrium's argument is set out in Figure 3.1.

Conclusion: a role for qualitative research

The options shown in Figure 3.1 are not so much alternatives as complementary questions which need to be answered in a particular sequence. As I shall show, this is because the main strength of qualitative research is its ability to study phenomena which are simply unavailable elsewhere.

Quantitative researchers are rightly concerned to establish correlations between variables. However, while their approach can tell us a lot about inputs and outputs to some phenomenon (e.g. counselling), it has to be satisfied with a purely 'operational' definition of the phenomenon and does not have the resources to describe how that phenomenon is locally constituted (see Figure 3.2). As a result, its contribution to social problems is necessarily lopsided and limited.

inputs → [the phenomenon] → outputs

Figure 3.2   The missing phenomenon in quantitative research

Moreover, when qualitative researchers use open-ended interviews to try to tap the perceptions of individuals, they too make unavailable the situations and contexts to which their subjects refer (see Figure 3.3).

perceptions → [the phenomenon] → responsees

Figure 3.3   The missing phenomenon in (some) qualitative research

The real strength of qualitative research is that it can use naturally-occurring data to locate the interactional sequences ('how') in which participants' meanings ('what') are deployed. Having established the character of some phenomenon, it can then (but only then) move on to answer 'why' questions by examining how that phenomenon is organisationally embedded (see Figure 3.4).

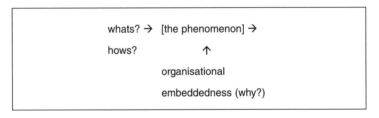

whats? → [the phenomenon] →

hows?   ↑

          organisational

          embeddedness (why?)

Figure 3.4   The phenomenon reappears

The kind of research outlined in Figure 3.4 can answer 'why' questions by locating the circumstantial limits of usage. This chapter has offered several examples of these limits: for instance, how cleft-palate surgeons need to find out their patients' 'true' feelings about their appearance; how HIV counsellors seek to establish their clients' risk status and not to explore the morality of their partners' actions; the ways in which positive thinking is a culturally approved way for cancer patients to define their outlook and the resources available to members of a children's group.

Almost twenty years ago, in a paper with Gubrium (Silverman and Gubrium, 1994), I argued that, unlike quantitative research, we delay 'why' questions in favour of 'what' and 'how' (for later thoughts by Gubrium, see Holstein and Gubrium, 2004). In this chapter, I have sought to develop that argument. Research which simply describes instances of perceptions is perhaps best left to the correlations available in survey research. By contrast, qualitative research can address the 'whats' and 'hows' of interaction. These 'whats' and 'hows' are to be found by studying the local management by participants of sequences of interaction which are themselves organisationally embedded.

In this chapter, we have travelled down a somewhat complicated path in order to understand how (the best) qualitative researchers attempt to make sense of their data. In doing so, I have introduced some fairly complicated ideas about what I have called 'sequential organisation'.

Jonathan Potter's comments early in this chapter reveal that commercial market research has little use for this kind of in-depth analysis and favours quick answers to (usually) uncomplicated questions. Commercial researchers and perhaps some student readers of these chapters may think that my appeal to esoteric thinkers like Sacks and Saussure may have ended up merely blinding you with science.

My task now remains to pull together the hints contained here that the kind of theoretically based data analysis I have described has some kind of practical input. In the next chapter, I will try to answer a relevant question: 'Where's the beef?'.

4

Applying Qualitative Research

Ethnographers have a closeness to the 'field' which is unavailable to quantitative researchers. This makes it almost inevitable that they will reflect on the impact of their research findings upon the people they study. Here are Jay Gubrium's thoughts on this matter following his research at Cedarview, the American residential home for disturbed adolescents discussed in Chapter 3:

> The 'findings' didn't so much reveal something about patients that was useful to them [the Cedarview staff] in their work, as it presented a portrait of what they – the staff – were up against themselves. Over and over again, they'd say, yes, that's right, that's what we have to do, especially at Cedarview. They recognized that they were representationally beholden to county welfare department sources (funding) and saw that I was showing what they were 'made' to do as a result of that. They were aware, in other words, of why they had to portray the kids the way they did and didn't much like that. Then again, at other times, in other contexts, they viewed what I had to say as too cynical, too much audience-oriented. There were real problems, in other words, and they were dealing with them effectively, or at least in one of the best ways anyone could.
>
> There's a story to be told about all my field stuff in this regard. I guess it's about time I, and maybe you and others, told it. We've all deconstructed their lives, but we haven't as much asked what the dynamics in place were doing for them as actors with investments in their performances. (Gubrium, Personal communication)

Following Gubrium, in this chapter I consider the 'story to be told' about the relevance of our kind of research. I begin by looking at the sometimes difficult wider context in which we seek to convince people of the applicability of qualitative research. This is followed by a discussion of fascinating findings based on qualitative research in two important, related, areas: organisational behaviour and practitioner–client relations. I then conclude by showing that, contrary to popular assumptions, policy relevant qualitative research is compatible with certain kinds of counting.

Gubrium himself has made out a strong case for the practical applicability of qualitative work, showing how good ethnography, by revealing the 'whats' and 'how' of institutional processes, can access phenomena that, as I put it in the previous chapter, 'escape' the gaze of quantitative research. In Case Study 4.1, Anne Ryen gives one example of how ethnography can make a direct link to practice.

Case Study 4.1   From the bush to business – making my research count!

These reflections refer to my work in East Africa across 15 years. For the past 5 years, I have been doing ethnographic work in business organisations run by Asians.

Based on my insights gained from my study, I have been recruited to the board of a private Norwegian company based in Uganda. The company is a regular business organisation competing in a tough private Ugandan market. The competition is hard and we compete with other international business organisations in the same line. Our business idea is estimated as having a very good market potential and the chances for generating a good fortune very likely.

The challenge turned out to be handling a start-up under circumstances with a continuous big discrepancy between budget and accounts accentuated by the fairly positive reports from our General Manager. We needed a constant reworking of our business idea which included three interlinked organisations, and to go out into the market asking for further investments from other capitalists (with big money) simply to handle the upcoming problems.

My data have given me a unique knowledge of running private businesses in the region with challenges that are ongoing. This has also affected field relations to an extent that I now draw upon my 'businesswoman' identity as a new way of communicating with people in the field. I have just received an invitation to start up a new business with one of them. So, applying my research has made a loop back to my project. This has informed both my work on the board and my field-work. (Ryen, Personal communication)

▬▬▬ The wider context

Unfortunately, in many societies, Ryen's hopeful message does not seem to have got across to bodies that fund or implement social research. Both 'push' and 'pull' factors have been important here. Policymakers and managers have been pushed away from ethnographic research because it takes a relatively long time to complete and appears to use unrepresentative samples. Even though some ethnographers are able to produce powerful arguments about what can be read from a single, well-researched, case (Flyvbjerg, 2004), others muddy the waters by political posturing and by suggesting that they want no truck with conventional scientific standards (see my discussion of postmodernism in Chapter 5).

The 'pull' of quantitative research is that it tends to define its research problems in a way that makes immediate sense to practitioners and administrators. First, unlike many qualitative researchers, quantitative people have few qualms about taking their variables (albeit 'operationalised') from current headlines (e.g. 'crime', 'poverty' or 'effective communication') or about speaking a scientific language of cause and effect. Second, precisely because quantitative research usually has little to say about how professional practice is enacted, it leaves such practice unexamined and hence unchallenged. By contrast, professionals are understandably quite protective when they find their own pet theories under the researcher's microscope. This situation is highlighted by Jonathan Potter's example:

> I guess in general terms we have been struck by a couple of things in trying to be more 'applied'. First, the experts may struggle with being researched as they are often trained in what they do using examples already constructed out of some earlier social science orthodoxy (counselling, psychoanalysis, whatever). They 'see' their own practices in these terms. Our Child Protection Officers working for a child charity (see Hepburn and Potter, 2004) are often reluctant to depart from some generalised (and individualised) version of psychoanalysis when they are talking about the calls.

> Second, it is very hard to undercut normative assumptions about people's practice. For example, when [in a study of focus groups] we looked at the moderation of expert moderators, the way they asked questions was notably different from all the manuals of focus group moderation. And the authors of those manuals were pretty reluctant to see our research as undercutting what they were claiming seemingly because it seemed sensible to them. (Potter, Personal communication)

Patient–doctor communication has probably been the major area of practice researched by social scientists. Undoubtedly the major research instrument in the field is a quantitative measure developed by Debra Roter, which allows a simple count of different communication 'events' (e.g. patients' questions). As John Heritage and Douglas Maynard (2006) have noted, 'the Roter system has served as the backbone for the study of the physician–patient relationship over the past 20 years'. Yet, as they observe, the Roter system 'is not without controversy'. In particular:

> Criticisms of the ... system have focused on the very features that have contributed to its success – its capacity to deliver an exhaustive and quantified overview of the medical encounter ... [Such] models take little account of the context or content of medical visits, sacrificing this for an overview across medical encounters in which the interactivity – the capacity for one party to influence the behavior of another, or to adjust behavior in response to another – becomes invisible. Hence, because the content or context of the interview is not assessed, these methods implicitly assume no connection between how people talk and either what they talk about or why they talk. ... Finally, general patient preferences may well vary in relation to illness conditions: A consumerist patient in the context of upper respiratory infections may look for a more paternalist stance than from a physician in the context of a cancer diagnosis. (Heritage and Maynard, 2006: 357–8)

Shortly, I will discuss Maynard's own trailblazing research on the organisation of news-telling in doctor–patient interaction. Unfortunately, even when demonstrations of the limitations of quantitative research are taken on board by policymakers, they do not usually turn to Maynard's kind of ethnographic research on the phenomenon itself. Instead, in many societies, the only kind of qualitative research that policymakers will commission are focus groups or 'exploratory' interview studies which, if successful, can form the basis of subsequent or revised quantitative surveys. By contrast to ethnographic research, these kinds of qualitative studies can produce results within a few days or weeks and thus offer the kind of 'quick fix' desired by research commissioners or proponents of the 'entrepreneurial university' (see https://webspace.utexas.edu/cherwitz/www/articles/gibb_hannon.pdf and www.youtube.com/watch?v=YrWNQXa5nBM).

Think, for instance, how focus groups have now become a major feature in how political parties orchestrate their election campaigns. The irony is that these relatively favoured techniques, as we saw in the previous chapter, share with quantitative research an inability to access the (practically important) topic of how institutions are routinely enacted.

Part of the problem arises from two dangerous orthodoxies that lie behind the thinking of many social scientists and policymakers who commission social research. The first orthodoxy is that people are puppets of social structures. According to this model, what people do is defined by 'society'. In practice, this reduces to explaining people's behaviour as the outcome of certain 'face-sheet' variables (like social class, gender or ethnicity). Let me call this the 'explanatory orthodoxy'. According to it, social scientists do research to provide explanations of given problems, such as why do individuals engage in unsafe sex? Inevitably, such research will find explanations based on one or more 'face-sheet' variables.

The second orthodoxy is that people are 'dopes'. Interview respondents' knowledge is assumed to be imperfect; indeed, they may even lie to us. In the same way, practitioners (like doctors or counsellors) are assumed always to depart from normative standards of good practice. This is the 'divine orthodoxy'. It makes the social scientist into the philosopher king (or queen) who can always see through people's claims and know better than they do.

What is wrong with these two orthodoxies? The explanatory orthodoxy is so concerned to rush to an explanation that it fails to ask serious questions about what it is explaining.

There is a parallel here with what we must now call a 'postmodern' phenomenon. I gather that visitors to the Grand Canyon in Arizona are now freed from the messy business of exploring the Canyon itself. Instead, they can now spend an enlightening hour or so in a multi-media 'experience' that gives them all the thrills in a pre-digested way. Then they can be on their way, secure in the knowledge that they have 'done' the Grand Canyon (for further comments on this phenomenon, see Percy, 2002).

This example is part of something far larger. In contemporary culture, the environment around phenomena has become more important than the phenomenon itself. So people tend to be more interested in the lives of movie stars than in the movies themselves. Equally, on sporting occasions, the crowd's Mexican Wave and pre- and post-match interviews with competitors become as exciting (or even more exciting) than the actual game. In the terms used in Chapter 3, in both cases, *the phenomenon escapes*.

This is precisely what the explanatory orthodoxy encourages. Because we rush to offer explanations of all kinds of social phenomena, we rarely spend enough time trying to understand how the phenomenon works. So, as I found when studying HIV-test counselling (Silverman, 1997), researchers may simply impose an 'operational definition' of 'unsafe sex' or a normative version of 'good counselling', failing to examine how such activities come to have meaning in what people are actually doing in everyday (naturally occurring) situations.

This directly leads to the folly of the divine orthodoxy. Its methods preclude seeing the good sense of what people are doing or understanding their skills in local contexts. It prefers interviews where people are forced to answer questions that rarely arise in their day-to-day lives. Because it avoids looking at these lives, it condemns people to fail without understanding that we are all cleverer than we can say in so many words. Even when it examines what people are actually doing, the divine orthodoxy measures their activities by some idealised normative standards, like 'good communication'. So, once again, like ordinary people, practitioners are condemned to fail.

In such an environment, qualitative research has become the 'poor relation', its most problematic forms serving, at best, as a handmaiden to its more respectable cousin who can express findings in numbers. Even when good ethnographic research with clear practical implications is funded and published, vested interests can mount an effective attack based on its 'doubtful' scientific legitimacy.

Like any rule, there are always exceptions. For instance, marketing research has accommodated a number of reasonably sophisticated qualitative methods and proved very acceptable to business (see Moisander and Valtonen, 2006). However, the more common response of animosity and resistance towards qualitative research is demonstrated in Case Study 4.2.

Case Study 4.2 The 'medical errors' controversy

In 2005 a highly prestigious medical journal (the Journal of The American Medical Association) published a study by the ethnographer Ross Koppel of a new software system which allowed computerised physician order entry (CPOE) of drug prescriptions in American hospitals (Koppel, 2005). This study arose by accident when Ross Koppel was doing research on the stress experienced by junior house physicians. It turned out that the CPOE system produced not only stress among these doctors but a noteworthy number of errors (although, as Koppel points out, some of these errors may not be experienced as stressful at the time). Moreover, although studies had been completed of how CPOE worked, these were generally quantitative and none was based on interviews and observations of these younger physicians.

To establish the extent of the phenomenon, Koppel constructed a multi-method study that incorporated face-to-face interviews and focus

(Continued)

(Continued)

groups with house physicians, shadowing doctors as they entered pre-scriptions into the system and observing nurses and pharmacists as they received prescriptions, interviews with senior medical and nursing staff and a 72-item questionnaire to a 90 per cent sample of house physicians. The prescribing errors discovered included doctors failing to stop one drug when they prescribed its replacement, confusion of which patient was receiving the drugs, and confusing an inventory list for clinical guidelines.

In the United States, it is estimated that medication errors within hospitals kill about 40,000 people a year and injure 770,000. According to Koppel's study, it turned out that CPOE systems can facilitate errors. Ironically, CPOE was most useful at stopping errors with few danger-ous consequences. In particular, the way in which CPOE had been pro-grammed had two unfortunate consequences: fragmented data displays meant that physicians had difficulty in identifying the specific patient for whom they were prescribing and the system did not work in the way that doctors worked and this created confusion or extra work to address the ambiguities.

Given the amount of government and industry support for CPOE, it is not surprising that Koppel's findings were treated as highly newsworthy by the national media but also came under immediate attack. Many medi-cal researchers suggested that such qualitative research could not pro-duce 'real data'. The manufacturers of CPOE systems launched a campaign which said that Koppel had 'just talked to people' and reported 'anecdotes'. In particular, the public were told, Koppel's study was faulty because it offered no measure of adverse drug events and had identified no 'real' errors but only 'perceptions of errors'. Critics also complained that he had studied an older CPOE system; that new systems have fixed all of those problems.

In response, Koppel and his colleagues made three arguments. First, they showed the limitations of previous research that had been used against them: 'Most of the research on CPOE was conducted to show its advantages over paper-based systems; almost all of the research was on reduction of potential rather than actual [adverse incidents]; many studies focused on physician satisfaction, barriers to acceptance, single outcomes, and very limited samples; several studies combine CPOE and clinical decision support systems, thus confounding the interpretation of CPOE's efficacy'. Second, Koppel and his colleagues argued that most of their critics had misunderstood the value of observing real-time medical decision making. Third, further research by Koppel does not support the claims that new CPOE systems have fixed all the problems.

Koppel's study is a fascinating example of what can happen when qualitative researchers stumble into what turns out to be a controversial topic. It reveals that the power of vested interests can work to denigrate qualitative research in support of a hidden agenda. In this way, the key strength of such an ethnographic study (its ability to depict what happens in situ) is presented as a weakness.

Central to this policy relevant, ethnographic work is the assumption that direct observation in situ (sometimes aided by recording devices) is the key to understanding how institutions function. This means that, as I argued in Chapter 2, other research methods such as interviews or focus groups cannot be treated as offering any sort of privileged access to how people actually behave.

Gale Miller and Kathryn Fox show that our concern with observation means that, unlike qualitative interviewers who are concerned with perceptions ('social worlds'), our focus is relentlessly on how institutions are constructed by their participants ('social settings'). As they put it:

> [T]he focus of discursively-oriented ethnographers' observations is different from those of other qualitative researchers. One way of understanding this difference is by considering what it means to study social settings versus social worlds. The latter research topic assumes that everyday life is organised within relatively stable and integrated ways of life ... Qualitative researchers of social worlds use observational and related methods to identify and reconstruct the perspectives and patterns of action and interaction that organise diverse social worlds. Discursively focused research on social settings, on the other hand, emphasizes how social realities are always under construction. It considers how setting members continually assemble and use the interactional and interpretive resources 'provided' by social settings to construct defend, repair, and change social realities. Hence the emphasis by discursively-oriented ethnographers on observing (directly, by means of audio and video recordings, and through the careful reading of texts) the actual ways in which setting members construct social realities by making sense of practical issues. (2004: 38)

In a single chapter, I cannot hope to do more than give you a small sense of the many practically relevant contributions made to society by what Miller and Fox call 'discursively focused research on social settings'. Therefore I have limited what follows to two important, related, areas:

- organisational behaviour and technologies
- practitioner–client relations.

Having discussed a few key studies in each area, I will show that, like most polarities (e.g. pure/applied research; manufactured/found data), the polarity between research that uses numbers and qualitative research can be taken too far. I will then conclude this chapter by returning to the kind of orienting themes upon which I have so far been touching.

Organisational behaviour and technologies

Ethnographic research, at its best, battles against what I have called 'the explanatory orthodoxy' in order to stop the phenomena of organisational life 'escaping'. As Gale Miller, Robert Dingwall and Elizabeth Murphy have noted, one of the major strengths of ethnographic research is that in-situ observation can lead to the identification of previously unnoticed 'best practices'. As they put it:

> '[B]est practices' [serve] to highlight qualitative researchers' distinctive vantage point for observing how solutions to organisational problems are often already evident in the everyday practices of organisation members. Ker Muir's (1977) discussion of the distinctive orientations and practices of professional police officers is an example of how qualitative researchers can identify best practices hidden by dominant problematic patterns, effective work within a troubled environment. Orr's (1996) study of copy machine technicians, on the other hand, shows how qualitative research can reveal widespread (but officially unrecognised and discouraged) best practices developed by organisation members in order to achieve organisational goals. (2004: 338)

Researchers who look for 'best practice' tread a slippery path. Should one follow Miller et al. and identify 'best practice' with the stated 'goals' of the organisation concerned? Alternatively, should researchers begin from their own normative standards (e.g. 'fair play', 'concern for the environment') and conduct an audit to see how far an organisation satisfies such standards?

Whatever stand we take on these matters of what *ought* to be, few can dispute the argument that debate about an organisation's behaviour is best served by knowledge of facts about what *is* the case. An excellent recent study of how employee appraisal schemes are enacted will serve as an example of how qualitative research can reveal a number of challenging facts about how organisations function.

Eva Nadai and Christoph Maeder (2006), two Swiss ethnographers, carried out a multi-sited ethnography consisting of case studies in three businesses (multinational company, retail group, bank) and three work integration programmes for the unemployed (a workshop for unskilled people, a training firm for office workers, and a youth program). Nadai and Maeder's data consisted of fieldnotes from around eighty days of site visits as well as many recorded interactions and interviews with managers and employees. For reasons of space, my discussion below omits their fascinating comparison of public and private organisations and instead focuses upon their findings about the three businesses.

Nadai and Maeder note that one of their three private firms, the multinational company they call 'Galactica', used a much more structured appraisal scheme than the other two companies. As they put it:

> Performance is *the* pervasive theme of GALACTICA's organisational culture. The company aims at becoming 'best in class', i.e. the top player in its branch, and consequently commits all its employees to the goal of 'excellence'. There is a highly sophisticated terminology regarding people's performance level, especially at the 'high' end of the performance scale, where we find such creatures as 'high potentials', 'high performers', 'must moves' and the like. Employees are assessed twice a year within a HR development cycle named DRIVE PROCESS, which is applied worldwide for employees and managers on every level, except the highest one. This model originates from the Harvard Business School with which GALACTICA cooperates very closely: every manager above a certain level must attend trainings specially designed and provided by this school for the company. The model distinguishes analytically two dimensions on a three-point nominal scale: performance and behavior. An employee can 'overachieve', 'achieve' or 'underachieve' the set goals on both axes. (2006: 9)

Below is how the appraisal model used at Galactica defines performance:

> An employee with at least one 1- rating is labeled a 'low performer'. Taken together all the fields containing a number one form a capital letter L, which stands for 'low' in general. Following this logic of distribution and attribution we find the high performing employees in any field with a three. The centre of the matrix is the 'good' or 'achieving' employee who neither over- nor underachieves. However, because in this logic the development of an employee is never allowed to stop, the requirements for a certain field in the matrix shift. This means that the system is used 'to raise the bar', to increase demands for performance and behavior every year for every single employee. Therefore, the sufficient level of this year will not be sufficient next

year. The principle of raising the bar is organised in a top down process: once a year the 'chief executive group' (CEG, i.e. the top stratum of the company) sets the 'top ten priorities' of the year. Managers then have to translate these priorities into practical goals of behavior and performance, and adapt it to the already existing claims and goals for the individual employees. This way a never-ending process of improvement is institutionalized. (Nadai and Maeder, 2006: 9)

The other two companies studied by Nadai and Maeder, Universum (a retail group) and Pecunia (a bank), have nothing like this complicated, Harvard Business School format of employee appraisal. As Nadai and Maeder note:

Whereas we encounter an elaborate terminology designating performance levels at GALACTICA for instance, UNIVERSUM and PECUNIA do not even have special terms for 'low' or 'high performers', save any nuances in between. And while 'performance' is *the* core concept for legitimizing HR procedures and wage systems at GALACTICA, the topic of 'cost reduction' fulfils a similar function at UNIVERSUM. At PECUNIA the introduction of an employee appraisal system is linked to the idea of a necessary modernization of organizational culture, but the company lacks a strong legitimation pattern regarding performance. (2006: 13)

Despite these difference performance measurement schemes, Nadai and Maeder note that, predictably, there was no one–one link between any given scheme and what actually happened in performance appraisals. In research interviews, 'even the seemingly simple three-point-scale of GALACTICA was interpreted differently by different informants. And most informants conceded that some aspects of performance cannot be determined unequivocally' (2006: 13).

What did this mean for how these different appraisal schemes were enacted, and what were the consequences of completed appraisals? Nadai and Maeder's ethnography shows six striking similarities between the three companies:

1   Although managers perceive inadequacies in the measurement schemes, Nadai and Maeder note that, when the same managers serve as appraisers, they act '*as if* an exact appraisal were possible, and draw on these assessments as objective facts that justify the corresponding treatment of employees. Thus, the objectivity assumption is consequential despite dissent'.

2   This meant that 'an individual's performance is believed to be the only legitimate determinant of his/her value for the company'. So appraisers act as if 'performance should entail positive or negative *consequences*'.

3   'In all three companies performance levels are assumed to follow the normal distribution across the whole workforce: there will be few "high" and few "low" performers with the vast majority of employees falling somewhere in between' (2006: 13).

4   Despite maintaining these working assumptions which fit their company's performance model, Nadai and Maeder note that a perceived poor performance may not be officially recorded. This is because 'supervisors may prefer not to label their subordinates as low performers, for instance when repeated insufficient performance of employees is partly attributed to their boss as well, or when the employee for some reason is regarded as irreplaceable.'

5   Even when a case of poor employee performance is recorded, the prescribed negative consequences may not follow. 'Our data strongly suggest that in this respect behavior is crucial: insufficient results may be tolerated, if the employee conforms to behavioral expectations' (2006: 14).

6   By contrast, perceived deficits on the behavioral dimension will usually lead to sanctions, softened by attempts to get the employees concerned to see the 'good sense' of what is happening to them – a process also used by confidence tricksters which the American ethnographer Erving Goffman (1959) vividly described as 'cooling the mark out'.

Nadai and Maeder's findings resonate with what Jill Jones and I discovered in a study of the Personnel Department of the Greater London Council 30 years earlier (Silverman and Jones, 1976). The (inevitable) gap between theory and practice, revealed by both studies, has clear implications for what are now called Human Resources Departments (a change of nomenclature which may in itself serve as a pre-emptive measure to 'cool the mark out').

The French social theorist, Michel Foucault, was fond of referring to systems as diverse as performance appraisal and prison governance as 'technologies'. However, in what follows, I will employ a more conventional usage which identifies 'technology' with mechanical systems ('hardware') and their operating structures ('software'). Let's look at one example of how ethnographers have examined new technologies.

Christian Heath and Paul Luff have observed that 'one of the most noticeable developments in personal computers in recent years has been the widespread deployment and use of graphical user interfaces. Rather than typing commands and instructions, users are presented with a range of devices, such as windows, icons, menus and cursors through which they operate the system' (2000: Ch. 6 Introduction).

Heath and Luff note that we have no clear understanding of why graphical interfaces appear to be easier to use by, for instance, architects. To find an answer, we need to go beyond conventional laboratory studies which focus on the activity and psychology of single individuals.

By contrast, Heath and Luff prefer to study people today in their ordinary work environments. As they put it, 'Rather than examining the conduct of users through experiments, we explore the use of a graphical user interface or "direct manipulation" systems in the accomplishment of everyday work' (2000: 201).

Heath and Luff's study was concerned with the ways in which architects use computers – especially recent computer-aided design (CAD) packages – in some cases in concert with other tools and artefacts, to make changes to particular plans and to coordinate their contributions with colleagues. Their research focused on the use of a CAD system in a medium-sized provincial architectural practice in England. Members of this practice use CAD systems to produce working drawings for contractors, to show clients what prospective buildings will look like and how they will fit into the landscape.

Heath and Luff's approach reveals much more than could ever be found in a laboratory. In particular, they show how, if we are to understand human–computer interaction (HCI), we must go beyond a simple focus on individuals. As they argue:

> [Our] observations point to the contingent organisation of system use, even when individuals work alone, and how the technology provides a resource in the design and development of buildings. It also reveals, once again, how system use is embedded in the mundane and indigenous competencies of the 'users'; competencies which in various ways arise in, and are preserved through, the interaction of the participants. (2000: 202)

The importance of observing how people interact with their fellow workers is underlined in Heath and Luff's study of videos of staff working in a control room which oversees the Bakerloo Line on the London Underground. In this control room are between four and six staff who oversee traffic movement and deal with problems and difficulties when they arise. Heath and Luff argue that the flexibility and emergent character of the staff's activities is far more complex and interactionally coordinated than could be formally prescribed in documents or training manuals.

A major factor is the mutual attention that staff pay to one another. As Heath and Luff put it:

[P]ersonnel within the Control Room organise their conduct so that whilst engaged in one activity, they simultaneously monitor or participate in the activities of others. This double-edged element of accomplishing these specialised tasks within the Line Control Room is an essential feature of their 'collaborative work', demanding that participants design their activities so that whilst undertaking one task they remain sensitive to the 'independent' actions of their colleague(s). (2000: 133)

The control room houses a line controller (LC) who coordinates the day-to-day running of the railway, a divisional information assistant (DIA) whose responsibilities include providing information to passengers through a public address (PA) system and communicating with station managers, and two signal assistants who oversee the operation of the signalling system on the busiest section of the line.

Heath and Luff show that the staff's need to monitor what each other is doing affects how they use objects like monitors and telephones:

Producing an activity whilst simultaneously participating in the activities of another, has implications for the ways in which personnel utilise the various tools and technologies within the Line Control Room. So, for example, the DIA may switch his CCTV monitor to a particular platform to enable him to read a number from the front of a train for the Controller, even though the DIA is engaged in delivering a public announcement and only happens to overhear that problems are emerging concerning the identity of particular trains. Or, for example, it is not unusual to find the Controller or DIA switching the telephone handset to the other ear, to enable his colleague to overhear a conversation with a member of the Underground staff based outside the Line Control Room. Almost all tasks within the Line Control Room are produced by the DIA or Controller as they simultaneously participate in the concurrent activities of their colleagues. The various tools and technologies which are provided to support these tasks, are shaped, corrupted and even abandoned, in order to enable Control Room personnel to participate simultaneously in multiple activities which more or less involve each other. (2000: 133–4)

An incident involving a train timetable shows how the control room staff maintain a sense of what each other is doing. Heath and Luff note that 'the timetable is not only a resource for identifying difficulties within the operation of the service, but also for their management' (2000: 133). Contingencies such as gaps between trains, absenteeism, vehicle breakdowns or the discovery of suspect packages often necessitate 'reformation' of the timetable varying from small adjustments to 'reformation' of the timetable; a process through which the LC reschedules trains and crews in order to maintain a coherent and even service. However, Heath and Luff observe that reforming the service is an extremely complex task, which is often undertaken during emergencies, and it is not unusual for the LC to have little time explicitly to keep his relevant colleagues informed.

Heath and Luff demonstrate a practical solution to this potential difficulty. LCs routinely

> render features of their individual reasoning and actions 'publicly' visible by talking though the reformations whilst they are being accomplished. The solution is analogous to the ways in which journalists handle the news in Reuters. The Controllers talk 'out loud', but this talk is not specifically addressed to a particular colleague within the Control Room. Rather, by continuing to look at and sketch changes on the timetable, whilst producing talk which is 'addressed' to oneself, the Controller avoids obliging anyone to respond. Talking through the timetable, whilst rendering 'private' activities publicly visible, avoids establishing mutual engagement with colleagues which would undermine the ongoing accomplishment of the task in question. (2000: 135)

Extract 4.1, in which the LC finishes one reformation and then begins another, shows how this talking 'out loud' is done in situ.

Extract 4.1   (Heath and Luff, 2000: Fragment 4.4, Transcript 1 adapted)

((...Controller (C) reads his timetable...))

C: It's ten seventeen to °hhhhhhh (4.3)

C: (Rr:) ri:ght (.) that's that one d<u>one:.</u>

C: hhh °hhh (.) hhh

C: Two: O: Six:: (.) For:ty Six:: (0.7)

C: Two Two Fi:ve

((...the DIA begins to tap on his chair and he and the trainee begin a separate conversation. As they begin to talk C ceases talking out loud...))

Here is what Heath and Luff say about this extract:

> Whilst looking at the timetable, the Controller announces the completion of one reformation and begins another. The Controller talks numbers, train numbers, and lists the various changes that he could make to the 206 to deal with the problems he is facing, namely reform the train to 246 or to 225. As the Controller mentions the second possibility, the DIA begins to tap the side of his chair, and a moment or so later, discusses the current problems and their possible solutions with a trainee DIA who is sitting by the DIA's side. As soon as the DIA begins to tap his chair and display, perhaps, that he is no longer attentive to his colleague's actions, the Controller, whilst continuing to sketch possible changes on the timetable, ceases to talk aloud. Despite therefore, the Controller's apparent sole commitment to dealing with specific changes to the service, he is sensitive to the conduct of his colleague, designing the activity so that, at least initially, it is available to the DIA and then transforming the way the task is being accomplished so that it ceases to be 'publicly' accessible. (2000: 137)

These and other data extracts (many involving video clips) reveal how staff in the control room simultaneously participate in, or attend to, the concurrent activities of their colleagues. This means that the systems with which they operate 'are shaped, corrupted and even abandoned, in order to enable Control Room personnel to participate simultaneously in multiple activities which more or less involve each other' (2000: 134).

This kind of detailed ethnography, influenced by CA's attention to the sequential organisation of interaction, has, of course, huge practical implications. Heath and Luff note that the series of three-week apprenticeships served by trainee controllers have a high failure rate. The varying contingencies that arise in operating the London Underground system produce a series of complicated work tasks which can only be successfully accomplished if systematically coordinated in real-time with the actions and activities of colleagues. Although they don't say so, I have no doubt that viewing Heath and Luff's videos could provide a significant resource in staff training.

Such a detailed study of the conduct of complicated work tasks depends upon a relentless emphasis on the way that employees use technologies in coordination with their colleagues. This emphasis can lead to practical inputs far wider than the usual focus with the study of HCI on how one employee uses a machine. As Heath and Luff conclude:

> The ways in which an individual's use of a particular tool or technology may be monitored by a colleague and feature in the production of

multiple activities, leads one to question, once again, the conventional wisdom in HCI which places the single user and their cognitive capabilities at the centre of the analytic domain. Noticing another's noticing of one's own conduct, and sensing that another's actions are sensitive to one's own actions and activities, informs the accomplishment of tool-mediated tasks in which an individual is engaged ... It is not simply that work within the Line Control Room is 'collaborative', it is rather that personnel, even within the accomplishment of apparently individual tasks, are sensitive to and participating in the activities of colleagues, and this participation is an intrinsic part of the organisation of the task. The use of the various tools and technologies in the Line Control Room features in the accomplishment of these various activities and their coordination, and provides resources through which potentially 'private' actions are rendered visible within the local milieu. (2000: 162–3)

The studies by Heath and Luff, Nadai and Maeder, and Koppel and his colleagues reveal the fine detail of how employees respond to particular technologies (e.g. the control room, CAD and CPOE packages) and organisational rules (e.g. job assessment criteria). Technologies and rules also impact on practitioner–client relations. However, while the organisation's clients (e.g. passengers on the London Underground and patients in receipt of drugs prescribed by physicians) are on the receiving end of employees' decisions, in the studies to which I now turn, clients are physically present and potential partners in making decisions.

Practitioner–client interactions

We saw earlier, in Koppel et al.'s research, how organisations may resist ethnographic findings which appear to threaten vested interests. We also know that organisational leaders can ignore research on their companies or, as happened in my research on the personnel function of a public sector organisation (Silverman and Jones, 1976), use the research as a legitimating device to support policies previously decided.

By contrast, independent practitioners appear much more open to research. Speculatively, I might suggest that this may relate to their self-perceptions as 'professionals' driven by a service ethic and to the fact that, because many practitioners work independently, they may not have observed others doing these tasks since they were trained.

All kinds of social science research seem to appeal, albeit in different ways, to practitioners. Quantitative approaches to, say, doctor–patient communication (such as Roter's rating scales) find a ready audience. Qualitative research based on interviews with clients also has a strong appeal, revealing things to practitioners that were unavailable in the consultation. For instance, Gubrium and his colleagues report a favourable response from practitioners to reports on how their patients responded to strokes (Gubrium et al., 2003). As Gubrium comments:

> [Our study] did have practical payoff in a few ways. First of all, when we reported back to the various health care providers (esp. PT, OT, rehab counselors, and rehab nurses) working with patients recovering from stroke and in rehabilitation, they said that the findings helped them to understand the various ways the patients respond to their stroke and to treatment. Some said it put 'compliance' in a new light. I recall one saying something like, now I understand what the patients are up against when they look ahead to their futures. (Gubrium, Personal communication)

Despite the insights offered by such interview studies in healthcare settings, there is no question of the huge appeal of ethnographic work based on observations of practice. I recall vividly the cries of recognition expressed by practitioners when I played them recordings of actual consultations in their field of expertise. Indeed, during feedback to practitioners from my research on paediatric consultations (Silverman, 1987) or HIV-test counselling (Silverman, 1997), their interest in taped consultations was enough to set off fascinating debates between themselves which often engrossed them so much that I barely had time to report my findings.

The vivid, revealing nature of such materials is reflected in Michael Bloor's comment that:

> In respect of other practitioners ... the qualitative researcher has the advantage that the research methods allow rich descriptions of everyday practice which enable practitioner audiences imaginatively to juxtapose their own everyday practices with the research description. There is therefore an opportunity for practitioners to make evaluative judgements about their own practices and experiment with the adoption of new approaches described in the research findings. Qualitative studies of everyday practice offer sufficiently detailed descriptions of practice to act as a spur to judgement and experimentation. If Schon (1983) is correct in his argument that professional work involves the deployment of knowledge-in-action rather than scientific knowledge, then qualitative research allows professional practitioners to reflect upon that, previously taken-for-granted, knowledge-in-action. (2004: 321)

In tune with Bloor's comments, the British sociologist Celia Kitzinger has used workshop sessions with practitioners to feed back findings on her conversation analytic (CA) research on telephone calls to a birth crisis helpline by women in crisis after giving birth (see Shaw and Kitzinger, 2005). In Case Study 4.3, you will find what she wrote to me in a personal communication about these sessions.

Case Study 4.3   CA for midwives

I have recordings of around 500 calls between about 300 callers and 5 different call-takers to a helpline for women in crisis after childbirth. I have permission to use these for research and training purposes.

I have used conversation analysis to make some 'collections' of common phenomena in the data. These include: a collection of empathetic receipts (a::::h, in a sympathetic tone of voice for example), a collection of continuers (mm hm), a collection of silences in different sequential positions (e.g. after a question and before an answer; in the middle of a turn), a collection of overlapping talk (some interruptive, some not), and collections of openings and closings, storytellings, reformulations of prior talk, corrections and so on.

[When you wrote to me] I was just off to run a training workshop for midwives, doulas, breastfeeding counsellors and antenatal teachers on how to interact sensitively with women they come across in the course of their work who have been traumatised by childbirth. I have been co-teaching two or three full-day workshops like this each year for the past three years, based on my ongoing research.

Here's how it works. Between 20–30 health professionals in the childbirth field attend the workshop. It begins with an introduction from my co-facilitator to post-natal post traumatic stress disorder (PN-PTSD) as a diagnostic category (symptoms, aetiology, treatment etc.), then moves on to the more general phenomenon of crisis/trauma/distress after childbirth, and how it is different from post-natal depression. Participants share their experiences of coming across women who are suffering this way and the difficulties they've had (e.g. 'she had a perfectly normal birth, she shouldn't have PTSD'; 'she's just angry with me all the time and explodes for no reason'; 'she refused even to try to breastfeed because she said the baby had caused her so much physical damage already').

The workshop participants are not trained counsellors and they often find women's anger and distress (at what should be a happy time in their lives since almost all have healthy live babies) difficult to understand or to deal with. After some discussion, they break into small groups for role play in which one takes the part of a woman with PN-PTSD, one the part of a 'listener', and the others observe and take notes about the process. They feed back to the main group about this experience.

Usually the following concerns are reported: how to start and end the interaction; how much 'advice' to give or whether 'listening' means keeping silent; how much it's okay to reveal about one's own experience or whether they should keep a professional distance; whether asking questions is intrusive or shows a proper interest; how to show empathy and caring without over-identifying with the distressed woman 'so we're both in floods of tears'; how to manage feelings of professional defensiveness when a woman is angry with her midwife/doula and the midwife/doula listening can hear that her co-professional did her very best under difficult circumstances and so on. Then we break for lunch.

After lunch I do a brief introduction summarising the issues participants have raised from the role play (tailoring it to the specifics of each group) and say that we're now going to work on some of those issues using not role play but recordings of actual interactions between distressed women and people trying to listen and help. (I also warn them that these can be distressing – they are pretty powerful calls.)

I usually start with 'openings'. Asking everyone to choose a partner, I tell them that I will play the beginning of an interaction and that I will switch the tape off after a few seconds and that one of them should take the role of the distressed woman and say whatever they would say next if they were the call-taker. I ask for feedback on what was said, we discuss the range of options and their pros and cons and we compare them with what the call-taker actually did say – for better or for worse – and the interactional consequences of that.

I usually move on to 'continuers', 'receipts' and 'reaction tokens'. I play a stretch of interaction and stop the tape each time the call-taker makes any noise at all: this includes 'mm hm', '.hhhh!', 'a:::h', 'mm', 'yeah' and so on. We discuss each one. I ask participants to consider: What's it doing there? How would the interaction be different if you substituted another minimal sound for this one? (I've also cut and pasted some 'fake' responses so they can hear why 'mm hm' is sometimes wrong in particular positions.) They are always very engaged and excited by this – everyone says how different it is from role play to deal with the 'real thing'.

(Continued)

(Continued)

I select from other collections depending on the needs of the group. I have a collection of women crying (which is something many people find difficult to deal with, especially when the tears make it impossible to hear the words clearly); a collection of 'delicate' talk about genitals and sexuality after childbirth (women lack the terminology to describe the parts of their genitalia that hurt, are scarred etc. – 'fanny' or 'down there' just isn't specific enough!); a collection in which the call-taker reveals personal information (it rarely works well); and so on.

I always end with a long sequence (6 minutes) from one of the most effectively handled calls in my collection. The call-taker leads the caller to a 'moment of revelation', and the caller subsequently sent a follow-up email thanking the call-taker and describing how she had now been able to take her child to the doctors for an injection without having a flashback to the operating table and 'freaking out'. It's an intensely moving and powerful call. I stop it at four or five points on the way through to ask for feedback or to get participants to say what they would say if they were the call-taker at this point and to discuss what's happening. We also use it to work on 'silence' (the good kind) since it has some outstandingly long silences (several of more than one second, one of 4 seconds and one of 6 seconds – before the 'moment of revelation'; compare Jefferson's (1973) finding that 1 second is the maximum permissible silence in ordinary conversation). We wrap it up with a discussion of the day overall and what people have learnt, and that's it.

Since running the workshops, I have been invited to become involved in the recruitment of participants for the Birth Crisis helpline. New recruits are asked to record the first 10 or so calls and to send them to me. I listen to them, identify some strengths and weakness, and talk them through with the novice call-taker who handled them. People have said they find this invaluable feedback.

Since starting to run the Birth Crisis workshops, participants at the workshop who work for other related helplines have asked whether I would be willing to record and analyse their calls and give feedback. I have collected and started work with students on calls from two other lines: the Home Birth helpline (Shaw and Kitzinger, 2005) and the Pelvic Partnership helpline (for women with *symphysis pubis* dysfunction). The idea with both Home Birth and Pelvic Partnership is to develop research and training in conjunction, and to offer my analyses back to the user groups, as well as developing academic publications. (Celia Kitzinger, Personal communication)

Kitzinger provides a thrilling example of how CA's close attention to the fine detail of how people interact can have considerable practical payoffs for practitioners. An Introduction to a recent special issue of the journal *Communication and Medicine* by the Finnish researchers Anssi Peräkylä, Johanna Ruusuvuori and Sanna Vehviläinen notes a number of such contributions:

> 'in settings where the institutional interaction involves a distinct interaction theory, conversation analytical research is in position where it can show whether or not, or to which degree, professional theories actually match empirical reality of professional–client interaction. (2005: 106)

Peräkylä and his colleagues go on to note that CA also has a great deal to say about how patients or clients behave. As they put it:

> Empirical interaction research can also explicate and give voice to the *clients'* orientations. Even when the professional theories emphasize issues such as 'patient centredness', these theories focus predominantly on the professionals' ways of interacting with the patients, without addressing the clients' interactional orientations. CA approach, however, gives us access to the clients' agendas. (2005: 107)

Peräkylä et al. recognise that when we introduce into research contextual factors, like 'cultural norms', we may start to tread on eggshells. As Schegloff (1991) argues, the issue of determining context is not a once-and-for-all affair because parties to an interaction continually work together at co-producing (and sometimes changing) some context. So we cannot explain people's behaviour as a 'response' to some context when that context is actively constructed (and re-constructed). This would be to retreat into the fallacy of what I called the 'explanatory orthodoxy'.

This means that we must not use the term 'context' lazily but actively study how participants construct contexts in real time. Such research will reveal that, for example, interaction with physicians is rarely limited simply to patients' commonsense assumptions about how doctors communicate, or to practitioners' own professional theories (e.g. how to take a 'history').

As Peräkylä et al. point out, 'Empirical interaction research has potential to analyse contextual features that participants orient to even when professional theory does not mention them' (2005: 106).

A brilliant illustration of this wider sense of context is to be found in a recent book by Douglas Maynard. Maynard (2003) uses CA methods to examine the organisation of the telling of 'good' and 'bad' news in medical consultations. His fascinating volume describes how the delivery of good and bad news interrupts our involvement in the taken-for-granted world. It shows how bad news is often forecasted in ways that are not separable from its telling and how such forecasting effectively procures a hearer's recognition of what is to come. This process is contexted within the author's original research on 'perspective–display sequences' in which the hearer's perspective is evoked in order to secure alignment to upcoming bad news. By contrast, good news is expected to come quickly.

Using data from paediatric settings, Maynard neatly demonstrates the adaptation of ordinary conversational practices in institutional talk. One such practice is to elicit an opinion from someone else before making one's own statement (see Extract 4.2).

Extract 4.2   (Maynard, 1991: 459)

1   *Bob:* Have you ever heard anything about wire wheels?

2   <u>Al:</u> They can be a real pain. They you know they go outta line

3   and—

4   <u>Bob:</u> Yeah the— if ya get a flat you hafta take it to a

5   special place ta get the flat repaired.

6   <u>Al:</u> Uh— why's that?

Notice how Bob's report (lines 4–5) is preceded by an earlier sequence. At lines 1–3, Bob asks Al on the same topic and receives an answer. Why not launch straight into his report?

Maynard suggests a number of functions of this 'pre-sequence':

1   It allows Bob to monitor Al's opinions and knowledge on the topic before delivering his own views.
2   Bob can then modify his statement to take account of Al's opinions or even delay such a statement by asking further questions of Al (using the 'chaining' rule).
3   Because Bob aligns himself with Al's proffered 'complaint' (about wire wheels) his statement is given in an 'hospitable environment' which implicates Al.

4   This means that it will be difficult (although not impossible) for Al subsequently to dispute Bob's statement.

Maynard calls such sequences a perspective–display series (or PDS). The PDS is 'a device by which one party can produce a report or opinion after first soliciting a recipient's perspective' (1991: 464). Typically, a PDS will have three parts:

- a question from A
- an answer by B
- a statement by A.

However, 'the PDS can be expanded through use of the probe, a secondary query that prefigures the asker's subsequent report and occasions a more precise display of recipient's position' (Maynard, 1991: 464).

In a paediatric clinic for children referred for developmental difficulties, the use of PDS by doctors is common. Extract 4.3 is one such example:

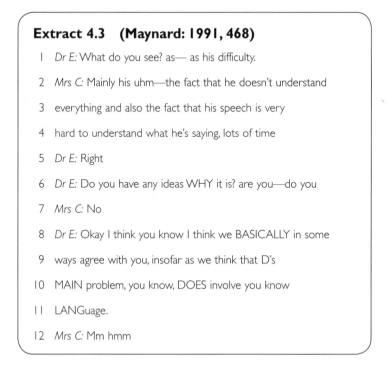

Extract 4.3   (Maynard: 1991, 468)

 1   *Dr E:* What do you see? as— as his difficulty.

 2   *Mrs C:* Mainly his uhm—the fact that he doesn't understand

 3   everything and also the fact that his speech is very

 4   hard to understand what he's saying, lots of time

 5   *Dr E:* Right

 6   *Dr E:* Do you have any ideas WHY it is? are you—do you

 7   *Mrs C:* No

 8   *Dr E:* Okay I think you know I think we BASICALLY in some

 9   ways agree with you, insofar as we think that D's

10   MAIN problem, you know, DOES involve you know

11   LANGuage.

12   *Mrs C:* Mm hmm

The basic three-part structure of the PDS works here as follows:

- Question (line 1)
- Answer (lines 2–4)
- Statement (lines 8–11)

Notice, however, how Dr E expands the PDS at line 6 by asking a further question.

As Maynard points out, doctors are expected to deliver diagnoses. Often, however, when the diagnosis is bad they may expect some resistance from their patients. This may be particularly true of paediatrics where mothers are accorded special knowledge and competence in assessing their child's condition. The function of the PDS in such an institutional context is that it seeks to align the mother to the upcoming diagnosis.

Notice how Dr E's statement in lines 8–11 begins by expressing agreement with Mrs C's perspective but then reformulates it from 'speech' to 'language'. Mrs C has now been implicated in what will turn out to be the announcement of bad news.

Of course, as Maynard notes, things do not always work out so easily for the doctor. Sometimes parents display perspectives which are out of line with the forthcoming announcement, for example by saying that they are quite happy with their child's progress. In such circumstances, Maynard shows how the doctor typically pursues a statement from the parent which acknowledges *some* problem (e.g. a problem perceived by the child's teacher) and then delivers his diagnosis in terms of that.

Maynard concludes that the PDS has a special function in circumstances requiring *caution*. In ordinary conversations, this may explain why it is seen most frequently in conversations between strangers or acquaintances where the person about to deliver an opinion is unlikely to know about the other person's views. In the paediatric setting discussed, the functions of the PDS are obvious:

> By adducing a display of their recipients' knowledge or beliefs, clinicians can potentially deliver the news in a hospitable conversational environment, confirm the parents' understanding, coimplicate their perspective in the news delivery, and thereby present assessments in a publicly affirmative and nonconflicting manner. (Maynard, 1991: 484)

In this way, we see how and why bad news is shrouded and good news is exposed in the context of historical and cultural variations and the deviant-case of HIV-counselling. This overall picture is delicately shaded by the author in relation to first-, second- and third-party news-telling and to how the messenger is treated. For example, in telling good news about oneself, one usually works to avoid the attribution of being engaged in self-praise. Equally, in telling bad news, 'blame negotiations' may arise.

Maynard seeks to position news-telling as a central feature of every-day life and of social interaction in general. In my view, he succeeds brilliantly. In the tradition of the nineteenth-century German sociolo-gist Georg Simmel, we come to see how an apparently trivial social form allows us to learn of the wider social fabric. Unlike Simmel, however, this work is supported by a massive amount of social research.

Ethnographers and social psychologists will be fascinated by the author's attempt to link CA to more conventional studies of 'informing'. Historians and anthropologists will be encouraged to think further about historical-cultural variations in news-telling in the light of the possible cultural universals implied here. Social theorists will not be disappointed by a volume that subtly weds empirical research to foundational state-ments by Husserl, Schutz and Garfinkel.

The attempt to reach out to such a wide range of academic posi-tions is praiseworthy. However, what is quite remarkable in such a scholarly volume is the extent to which Maynard is able to draw in two quite different audiences. If there still remains any trace of that mythical beast 'the general reader', that creature will surely be fasci-nated by much of this volume. Almost uniquely in an academic work, Maynard begins with a chapter that is built around compelling exam-ples from all our everyday experiences captured in his phrase 'flash-bulb memory'. All the other chapters start with a vivid quote from everyday life. In these and other ways, this volume is the antithesis of a dry, academic work and should make compelling reading to non-specialists.

In terms of the concerns of this chapter, Maynard's book is also very useful to a further non-academic audience. I refer to medical practition-ers, counsellors and, indeed, to the 'psy' professions in general. Such readers are fortunate both that Maynard has conducted considerable research in clinical settings and that he is so adept at orienting towards practitioners' practical concerns. A section on the usually stoic response to the receipt of bad news will simply be required reading for these people. Indeed, I believe that Maynard's discussion of asymmetries in good and bad news-telling in clinical settings is destined to become required reading in medical schools. In the following example you will find Maynard's own comments on the applicability of the research discussed in his book:

> There is an epilogue to my book in there that is unabashedly applied. The epilogue is called 'How to Tell the News.' Further, I give talks to clinicians on just that topic with some degree of regularity (In U.S. medical schools, these are called 'grand rounds'). The clinicians become very engaged when they see and hear actual episodes, and they usually have their own anecdotes and experiences to talk about. Their remarks are 'touched off' by my presentation, and in turn 'touch off' more things that I can say in relation to the CA research I've done. I emphasize that CA research is based on systematic inquiry that can provide a kind of validity check for anecdotal reports. (Maynard, Personal communication)

Maynard's work shows how medical encounters may, in part, involve the use of mechanisms, like the PDS, which occur in ordinary conversation. By using such conversation as a baseline, CA allows us to identify what is distinctive about institutional discourses.

In addition, a distinctive contribution of CA is to ask questions about the *functions* of any recurrent social process. So Maynard examines how his PDS sequences work in the context of the delivery of bad news. It also follows that his work achieves considerably more than out-of-context ideological critiques of medical practice which tend to cast doctors as mere tyrants or spokespersons for capitalist interests (see Waitzkin, 1979).

Taken together, the work discussed in this section contains a number of lessons about how qualitative researchers can contribute to a debate about best practice. In particular:

- Researchers ought not to begin from normative standards of 'good' and 'bad' communication. Instead the aim should be to understand the skills that participants deploy and the functions of the communication patterns that are discovered.
- While qualitative interviews can reveal to practitioners unknown aspects of clients' perceptions, there is no substitute for research focused on the fine detail of actual practitioner–client interaction and the various contexts which they make relevant.
- Playing back tapes and videos of interactions involving themselves and colleagues gives practitioners new insights into their own practice.

The kind of dialogue presupposed in these lessons precludes the know-it-all tendency of what I earlier called the 'divine orthodoxy'. The focus on 'how' questions also contests the assumptions of the 'explanatory ortho-doxy' that we must rush to look for causes and correlations.

However, it would be foolish to suppose that everything is just a matter of interaction between practitioners and their clients. For instance, in my research on HIV-test counselling, I noted how the communication meth-ods of counsellors were often sorely constrained by the limited time they had available for each patient interview.

This matters because there is no point in suggesting reforms in how practitioners communicate when the social context pressures them in a particular direction. Such an intervention can only be irrelevant and even elitist. Instead, by appreciating the skills of practitioners, in the context of the demands made upon them, we can open up a fruitful debate about *both* communication and the social and economic constraints on com-munication.

However, for a debate to be successful, we must find responsive audi-ences. While workshops based on tapes of actual client consultations provide compelling material, it is unrealistic to assume that we can reach a substantial audience by workshops alone. In the following section, I consider ways of analysing data and reporting research that will speak to practitioner audiences.

Writing qualitative research with numbers

As I suggested at the beginning of this chapter, numbers count with prac-titioners and policymakers. Are numbers always ruled out in qualitative research – nothing more than a kind of 'sell out' to an environment that demands that you assign a numerical value to every observation? Alternatively put, are there types of quantification which can actually aid ethnography and CA?

My positive answer to this question is grounded in my belief that quan-tification can sometimes help us sort fact from fancy and, thereby, improve the validity of qualitative research. There are two broad ways in which simple counting techniques are effective:

- as an initial means of obtaining a sense of the variance in the data (Type 1)
- at a later stage, after having identified some phenomenon, checking its prevalence (Type 2).

As an example of Type 1 tabulations, I will take a study of calls to a child protection hotline. As in my own study of HIV-test counselling

(Silverman, 1997), Hepburn and Potter found that practitioners working for the UK National Society for the Prevention of Cruelty to Children (NSPCC) were fascinated to hear tapes of their (and others')
practice. As they put it:

> One of the limitations of training for work of this kind is that it is
> often based on idealizations or suppositions about the way interac-
> tion works ... One thing we found with this project was that the ini-
> tial practical input was rather simple. We were able to provide Child
> Protection Officers (CPOs) with a set of digitised and roughly tran-
> scribed calls on a CD that they could play in their own PC (stopping
> and starting, dipping into and so on). Some of the CPOs found that
> the facility to reflect on her or his own practice was very helpful. We
> hope that toward the end of the research we can provide more sophis-
> ticated training aids which allow CPOs to step through digitised calls
> with analytic observations and suggestions about them (e.g. about
> trouble and its solution). The aim of these kinds of practical interven-
> tions here is not to tell the CPOs how to do their job better, but to
> provide one sort of resource that they can draw in their training and
> practice as is helpful. (2004: 194–5)

However, Hepburn and Potter did not just record and replay tapes but
offered practitioners insights into their analysis of the data. In part, this
involved identifying various phenomena and then using simple tabulations to establish the degree of variance of some phenomenon.

For instance, Hepburn and Potter discovered that callers to this helpline
tended to preface their reports with a reference to their 'concerns'. So a
typical call would begin: 'I'm concerned about X'. In order to check the
prevalence of this phenomenon, the researchers did a range of simple
counts as an aid to understanding the patterning of the way constructions
using the terms 'concerned' and 'concern' were used. This is how
Hepburn and Potter explain their approach:

> [I]t was interesting to consider how specific to the NSPCC data
> concern constructions were. To check this we did something very
> simple, which was to compare prevalence in the NSPCC calls with
> a corpus of everyday phone calls. The terms 'concern' and 'con-
> cerned' appear an average of 7 times per call in our material, but
> only 0.3 times per call in the (everyday) corpus. At a more specific
> level we were interested in the prevalence of concern constructions
> in the call openings, and also how many were initiated by the caller
> and how many by the CPO. About 60 per cent of openings use

concerned constructions, about two thirds of these were initiated by the caller, and about a third by the CPO. (2004: 189)

Such tabulations at an early stage of a qualitative study can only be suggestive. They are not the endpoint but a signpost to further work. As Hepburn and Potter put it:

> These counts were certainly interesting, and highlighted some things to follow up. But their implications are not conclusive on their own. Indeed, they are most unclear without considering the specifics of the interaction and how it unfolds. The course of analysis works through developing ideas about what is going on in some materials ('hypotheses' in rather grander methods speak) and exploring them, seeing how far they make sense. (2004: 189)

What I have called Type 2 tabulations are used at a later stage of the research after a clear phenomenon has been identified. In this context, quantification can neatly tie in with the logic of qualitative research when, instead of conducting surveys or experiments, we count participants' own categories as used in naturally occurring places. Let me give you an example of this.

In the early 1980s (see Silverman, 1987: Chs 1–6) I was directing a group of researchers studying a paediatric cardiology (child heart) unit. Much of our data derived from tape-recordings of a weekly outpatient clinic.

We soon became interested in how decisions (or 'disposals') were organised and announced. It seemed likely that the doctor's way of announcing decisions was systematically related not only to clinical factors (like the child's heart condition) but also to social factors (such as what parents would be told at various stages of treatment). For instance, at a first outpatients' consultation, doctors would not normally announce to parents the discovery of a major heart abnormality and the necessity for life-threatening surgery. Instead, they would suggest the need for more tests and only hint that major surgery might be needed. They would also collaborate with parents who produced examples of their child's apparent 'wellness'. This step-by-step method of information-giving was avoided in only two cases. If a child was diagnosed as 'healthy' by the cardiologist, the doctor would give all the information in one go and would engage in what we called a 'search and destroy' operation, based on eliciting any remaining worries of the parent(s) and proving that they were mistaken.

By contrast, in the case of a group of children with the additional handicap of Down's Syndrome, as well as suspected cardiac disease, the

Table 4.1   First history taking question – Down's Syndrome children

Is he/she well?	0
From your point of view, a well baby?	1
Do you notice anything wrong with him/her?	0
Does he/she get breathless?	1
Does he/she get a few chest infections?	1
How is he/she?	6
Question not asked	1
Total	10

Source: adapted from Silverman, 1981

doctor would present all the clinical information at one sitting, avoiding a step-by-step method. Moreover, atypically, the doctor would allow parents to make the choice about further treatment, while encouraging them to dwell on non-clinical matters like their child's 'enjoyment of life' or friendly personality.

This medical focus on the child's *social* characteristics was seen right at the outset of each consultation. I was able to construct a table, based on a comparison of Down's and non-Down's consultations, showing the different forms of the doctor's questions to parents and the parents' answers.

Table 4.1 looked quite unremarkable – just the sort of questions you would expect a cardiology physician to ask parents at a first consultation. It was only when we compared these questions with the question format with non-Down's children that something striking surfaced.

Tables 4.1 and 4.2 show a strong tendency with Down's children for the doctor to avoid using the word 'well' about the child. At my heart

Table 4.2   First history-taking question – random sample from the same clinic

Is he/she well?	11
From your point of view, a well baby?	2
Do you notice anything wrong with him/her?	1
From the heart point of view, is he/she active?	1
How is he/she?	4
Question not asked	3
Total	22

Source: adapted from Silverman, 1981

clinic, the most common question that the doctor asked parents was: 'A well child?'. However, parents of Down's Syndrome children were rarely asked this question. Instead, the most common question was: 'How is he/she?'. Note that the categories in the tables were not my own; I simply tabulated the different questions as actually given (just as Hepburn and Potter tabulated the participants' use of the word 'concern').

Further analysis revealed that parents collaborated with the doctor's choice of words, answering in terms like 'alright' and 'fine' rather than 'well'. This absence of reference to 'wellness' proved to be crucial to understanding the subsequent shape of the clinic consultation.

Having compared medical history-taking with Down's and non-Down's families, we moved on to the final stage of these consultations to examine how treatment decisions were arrived at. In the early 1980s, a child with symptoms of congenital heart disease would usually be recommended for cardiac catherisation, a diagnostic test requiring a brief stay as an inpatient.

In these cases, the doctor would say to the parents something like:

'What we propose to do, if you agree, is a small test.'

No parent disagreed with an offer which appeared to be purely formal – like the formal right (never exercised) of the Queen not to sign legislation passed by the British Parliament. For Down's Syndrome children, however, the parents' right to choose was far from formal. The doctor would say things to them like:

'I think what we would do now depends a little bit on parents' feelings.'

'Now it depends a little bit on what you think.'

'It depends very much on your own personal views as to whether we should proceed.'

Moreover, these consultations were longer and apparently more democratic than elsewhere. A view of the patient in a family context was encouraged and parents were given every opportunity to voice their concerns and to participate in decision making.

In this sub-sample, unlike the larger sample, when given a real choice, parents refused the test – with only one exception. Yet this served to reinforce rather than to challenge the medical policy in the unit concerned. This policy was to discourage surgery, all things being equal, on such children. So the democratic form co-existed with (and was indeed sustained by) the maintenance of an autocratic policy.

The research thus discovered the mechanics whereby a particular medical policy was enacted. The availability of tape-recordings of large numbers of consultations, together with a research method that sought to develop hypotheses inductively, meant that we were able to develop our data analysis by discovering a phenomenon for which we had not originally been looking – discovery which is far harder to make in more structured quantitative research designs.

'Democratic' decision making or 'whole-patient medicine' are thus revealed as discourses with no intrinsic meaning. Instead, their consequences depend upon their deployment and articulation in particular contexts. So even democracy is not something that we must appeal to in all circumstances. In contexts like this, democratic forms can be part of a powerplay.

Two practically relevant matters arose from the study of Down's Syndrome consultations. First, we asked the doctor concerned to rethink his policy or at least reveal his hidden agenda to parents. We did not dispute that there are many grounds to treat such children differently from others in relation to surgery. For instance, they have a poorer post-surgical survival rate and most parents are reluctant to contemplate surgery. However, there is a danger of stereotyping the needs of such children and their parents. By 'coming clean' about his policy, the doctor would enable parents to make a more informed choice.

The second practical point, revealed by this research, was to show that we should not assume that any particular communication technique always works in the same way whatever the context. My relativistic stance about 'patient-centred medicine' rightly serves to discomfit liberal doctors wedded to this fashionable orthodoxy. For, as good practitioners realise, no style of communication is intrinsically superior to another. Everything depends upon its context.

These two examples (Down's Syndrome children in a cardiology clinic and Hepburn and Potter's study of calls to a child protection helpline) show that there is no reason why qualitative researchers should not, where appropriate, use quantitative measures. Simple counting techniques, theoretically derived and ideally based on participants' own categories, can offer a means to survey the whole corpus of data ordinarily lost in intensive, qualitative research. Instead of taking the researcher's word for it, the reader has a chance to gain a sense of the flavour of the data as a whole. In turn, researchers are able to test and to revise their generalisations, removing nagging doubts about the accuracy of their impressions about the data.

This shows that well-grounded, simple tabulations can improve the quality of qualitative research and speak to practitioners who are used to seeing research expressed numerically. A recent study of US general practice consultations by John Heritage and colleagues (2006) underlines this point in spades (see the extracts from their paper in Box 4.1). The study reveals that the standard medical consultation can, in unforeseen ways, fail to meet patients' concerns.

Box 4.1   Meeting patients' unmet concerns (Heritage et al., 2006: 1–9)

According to the National Ambulatory Medical Care Survey, about 40% of patients bring more than one concern to primary, acute-care visits. Some studies suggest that, when given the opportunity, patients raise an average of three concerns per visit. However, physicians' opening questions (e.g. What can I do for you today?) normally elicit only a single concern, and the expression and exploration of additional concerns is frequently abbreviated, if not absent.

Given that the average primary-care visit is constrained to about 11 minutes in family practice, and that new and potentially severe concerns can emerge late in visits, physicians may face difficulties in completely and effectively managing the full array of patients concerns ...

This study tests two question designs that implement the recommended survey of additional concerns to determine if, when asked at the recommended time, they reduce the incidence of patients' unmet concerns. It also examines the impact of these questions on visit length, and on the proliferation of concerns that were unanticipated by patients before visits but contingently produced in response to the study questions.

Two types of question design

It has long been known that the design of Yes/No questions frequently communicates an expectation in favor of either 'Yes' or 'No' responses. For example, the following questions, drawn from an actual visit, all favor 'No' responses:

DOC: --> And do you have any other medical problems?

PAT: Uh No.

        (7 seconds of silence)

DOC: --> No heart disease?

(Continued)

(Continued)

PAT: ((cough)) No.

          (1 second of silence)

DOC: --> Any lung disease as far as you know?

PAT: No.

One element of this communication process is to be found in words that are recognized by linguists to have positive or negative polarity. For example, the word 'any' is negatively polarized: it ordinarily occurs in declarative sentences that are negatively framed (e.g., 'I haven't got any samples'), and is normally judged to be inappropriate in positively framed declarative sentences (e.g., 'I've got any samples.'). By contrast, the word 'some' is judged appropriate in positively framed sentences (e.g., 'I've got some samples'), and inappropriate in negatively framed ones (e.g., 'I haven't got some samples').

Although both 'some' and 'any' can appropriately be used in questions, their polarized associations may have a direct causal influence that biases responses. This study tests for this effect in relation to the question 'Is there [some/any]thing else you would like to address in the visit today?'

Intervention

After physicians had performed four visits in a normal fashion, they were randomly assigned to one of two intervention conditions for all remaining observations. Physicians watched a 5-minute video recording that described, explained, and exemplified the communication intervention. The recording required physicians to open visits in their usual way and, once the presenting concern was determined, to ask 'Is there anything else you want to address in the visit today?' (ANY condition) or 'Is there something else you want to address in the visit today?'(SOME condition) ...

Forty nine percent of the sample listed more than one concern in the pre-visit survey (Mean 1.7; SD 0.9; Range 1–6). In the recorded visit, 53% of patients presented more than one concern (Mean 1.9; SD 1.0; Range 1–5). Compared to other controls, patients who were not asked to list their reasons for the medical visit in the pre-visit survey did not significantly differ in the number of presented concerns, indicating that the pre-visit survey did not have a priming effect (p=0.998).

The primary analysis of the intervention was restricted to patients who listed two or more pre-visit concerns (n=100). In the control condition (n=36), 42% of patients left visits with at least one unmet concern, compared to only 24% of patients in the SOME condition (n=29).

Forty-three percent of patients in the ANY condition (n=35) left with unmet concerns.

Unmet patient concerns can leave unaddressed medical problems to worsen, contribute to unnecessary patient anxieties, or result in additional visits that are costly in terms of patient time and limited medical resources. While textbooks on medical interviewing recommend surveying patients' additional concerns early in visits with questions such as 'Do you have any other concerns you would like to discuss today?', our results suggest that this recommendation, if followed to the letter, will not reduce the incidence of patients' unmet concerns. However, a comparatively simple modification of this question to 'Do you have some other concerns you would like to discuss today?' may nearly halve the incidence of patients' unmet concerns.

Concluding remarks

In some respects, this chapter has followed an all-inclusive approach rather like that rare example of apparent liberalism in Mao Tse Tung's China which went under the title 'Let a Thousand Flowers Bloom'. Among other things, I have suggested that, in order to improve the practical relevance of good qualitative research:

- the intelligent use of counting can speak to practitioners and policy-makers as well as improving research validity
- ethnography can reveal fascinating, practically relevant things about organisational routines
- CA can show the fine detail of interaction and sometimes reveal to practitioners skills that they didn't even know they possessed (see, in particular, Peräkylä, 1995).

However, there is one point that emerges from these matters that needs underlining. It is the thought I would like to leave with you. Namely, writing is always for an *audience*. Too easily, in later life, one takes from a college degree the assumption that writing is just about appealing to one person (your professor) and so getting a good grade. Even if you are lucky enough to go on to postgraduate study and even to get a university post, you continually need to remind yourself that fellow academics are only one of several potential audiences. At some stage, in some way, your audience should include policymakers and practitioners and (barely dealt with in this chapter) lay audiences. However, although recognising that there are such audiences out there is a necessary first step, by itself it is insufficient. Each group will only want to hear about your work if it relates to their needs. So you must understand where such groups are 'coming from' and write in a manner, both in terms of form and content, that speaks to concerns which you share with them. This means implementing a skill which we use all the time in everyday life (i.e. relating current audience expectations to the way we issue an invitation or break bad news). CA calls this skill 'recipient design'.

In the final analysis, if you want to succeed in your research and beyond, you will have to be responsive to the various audiences who might be prepared to listen to what you have to say. As in so many other aspects of life, people who complain about the 'cruel world' are often the very people who disdain the occasionally difficult but generally rewarding business of listening to what others are saying.

5

The Aesthetics of Qualitative Research: On Bullshit and Tonsils

In the previous chapter, I discussed the contribution that qualitative research can make to society. In this chapter, I move from what qualitative research *does* to the more fundamental question of its nature, that is, what qualitative research *is*, quite apart from any contribution to society (or elsewhere) that it makes.

So I shall ask: in what ways does our kind of research demand attention and claim to be of value for what it is, not necessarily for what it does? This is how I am using the word 'aesthetics'. It will mean that we will be looking at the claims that contemporary qualitative research makes about itself. Take the call for help by a student on an internet site shown in Box 5.1.

Box 5.1 Identity in the refrigerator

I am currently completing a project for an architecture course where [I am] examining the refrigerator as a means of addressing issues of place and identity. This is a map-making exercise whereby I must generate maps of complex relationships that are not easily apparent by mapping the contents of the fridge. The following are for consideration:

- The fridge becomes a reliquary for contemplation of that which is to become oneself.
- The fridge defines an anthropological dig precipitated by a meal and carried out at a frenzied pace.
- The fridge frames one's Arcimboldian portrait(s) of lifestyle choices.
- The fridge is a fetishistic totem of domestic status, often as empty of meaning as it is of nutrition.
- The fridge is a cryogenic chamber of suspended alimentary decay.

Does anyone know of publications/articles that address the refrigerator as a reflection of identity? I'm also interested in any paintings, drawings, collages etc. that might address this topic. Please email me directly.

This student research project (passed on to me by Anne Murcott) will serve as an example of the things that concern me about our field. It raises a number of questions. First, why is such complicated jargon being used in defining her research problem (e.g. 'reliquary', 'Arcimboldian', 'totem', 'cryogenic chamber')? Why not simply work inductively and say that you are interested in how people use their refrigerators? Then you can study what they do and report what comes up, recognising that 'identity' may not be part of it.

Second, bear in mind that this is only a student project. How did architecture courses become involved in the kind of highfalutin' theory and jargon displayed here? Why are architects trained in looking for obscure literature and not, apparently, encouraged to study how people actually behave in the real world? As we will see later, I believe part of the answer lies in the way in which a particular approach (postmodernism) has come to privilege grand theory and experimental writing at the expense of sober enquiry and a concern for truth.

In this respect, social science is only a little behind what happened in literary studies. At a conference of the Modern Language Association, David Lehman recalls being told:

> If you want to make it in the criticism racket, you have to be a deconstructionist, or a Marxist or a feminist. Otherwise, you don't stand a chance. You're not taken seriously. It doesn't matter what you know or don't know. What counts is your theoretical approach. And this means knowing jargon, and who's in and who's out. (1991: 52, quoted in Benson and Stangroom, 2006: 151–2)

The philosophers Ophelia Benson and Jeremy Stangroom refer to this need to display jargon as a 'peacock's tail syndrome'. As they put it:

> As Theory gained a foothold in the academy, it became necessary for ambitious young academics to compete on a terrain which it defined. The more Theory dominated, the fiercer the competition became, which meant that if scholars wanted to be noticed, they had to engage in increasingly ostentatious displays of theoretical virtuosity. In the end, driven by a positive feedback loop, display became everything: the peacocks had colonised the world of literary studies. (2006: 154)

Of course, this is not to deny that theory has a crucial role to play in research. However, as I have argued elsewhere (Silverman, 2010, 2011), theoretical thinking should be an aid to sober, empirical research – not its replacement.

As should by now be apparent, in this chapter, I will offer my own diagnosis of contemporary qualitative research. As you read what follows, you may note a change of tone from the rest of this book. For instance, the previous chapter was intentionally measured and sober. By contrast, this chapter, implied by its subtitle, may strike some readers as outrageous or, perhaps, quirky. This is equally intentional.

Throughout this book, we have seen that 'qualitative research' is a contested zone. But, as you will discover, when it comes to aesthetics, it is nothing less than a minefield where trenchant positions are the order of the day. So this penultimate chapter is an attempt at a clear statement of what I believe to be right and wrong among these conflicting arguments.

Now a word about my subtitle. I will, for the moment, keep tonsils up my sleeve or perhaps at the back of my throat. But what about 'bullshit'? Let me approach my use of this term in an indirect fashion.

'Bullshit' is a modern term: in Europe 100 years ago it was, I think, largely unknown. However, there was a word around with a similar usage. The word 'kitsch' was commonly used in late-nineteenth century Vienna to describe pretentious political and cultural forms. We learn from Janik and Toulmin's (1996) marvellous book *Wittgenstein's Vienna* that the Habsburg Emperor of Austro-Hungary signed himself 'K und K' (*kaiserlich und königlich* or 'imperially and kingly'). 'K und K' was the basis for 'Kakania', the term that the novelist Robert Musil used to signify Vienna 100 years ago when Imperial pretensions were not supported by a crumbling Empire. Incidentally, you ought to know that 'Kaka' is a euphemism for 'shit', so we already see a link with 'bullshit'!

The philosopher Wittgenstein, whom we first encountered in Chapter 1, was another product of late-Habsburg Vienna. He satirised the overblown claims of philosophers as well as (incidentally) the overblown music of Gustav Mahler (which draws upon the same romantic and emotionalist themes that, as I will later show, characterise much contemporary qualitative research).

Almost one hundred years after Mahler and the Habsburgs, the Czech novelist Milan Kundera, in his book *The Unbearable Lightness of Being* (2004), discusses the politics of kitsch, showing how the old socialist regimes of Eastern Europe constructed subjects who were always marching and parading in much the same way as the Nazi-era Nuremburg Rallies. In the post-Communist world of Kundera's later novel *Immortality*, people still march but the banners are more likely to show Donald Duck and Micky Mouse than Karl Marx and Friedrich Engels. Disney has replaced Marx but kitsch lives on and the spectacle is no less political.

By the beginning of the present century, in a unipolar world, the American Empire has replaced the Soviet, Nazi and Habsburg Empires. So let's replace the Habsburg word 'kitsch' with the American term 'bullshit'. Harry Frankfurt (2005) has discussed the origin of this word using dictionaries but I rather like Eric Whittle's observations on what 'bullshit' means in the Australian outback presented in Box 5.2.

Box 5.2   Bullshit in the outback

Of all the definitions of 'bullshit' read so far, I've yet to find one that discusses the source himself – the bull. I'm speaking from many years experience of working with, and observing, wild cattle in our far North. Like the males of other animal species, wild bulls often fight over harem rights. Typically they go through a display routine something akin to 'come any closer, and I'll punch your lights out!'. There's a lot of bluffing, swaggering, mouthing off, and literally bullshitting. The process might go on for minutes or hours, but all the while the bulls are constantly dribbling shit from the back end and paddling it around with their tail. You can always tell when a bull is in fighting mode because his arse-end is smothered in green slime. They circle around each other with their noses down, pawing up as much dust as they can (think 'bulldust'), bawling each other out and sniffing at each other's shit. Does that sound like some academic discussions you've witnessed! The point is, the issue of who wins is most often settled in these preliminaries. The process might go on for a while, but one or the other has already conquered, without the potential danger of actually locking horns. One short rush and it's all over. In conversations among the stockmen, use of the term 'bullshit' was almost invariably in this context. If someone was suspected of bluffing/boasting/overstating their ability to ride, root, drink or fight, then he was 'full of bullshit' or 'bullshitting' or simply dismissed with 'Ahh bullshit!'. (Eric Whittle, Personal correspondence)

Eric Whittle hints at what bullshit looks like in academia. I will shortly return to this issue. For the moment, I want to consider how bullshit suffuses popular culture and politics. Here 'bullshit' denotes a world in which aesthetics reduces to celebrity and lifestyle. A world in which supposedly 'serious' newspapers are dominated by lifestyle columns telling us how to live our lives and in which politicians must have an attractive 'personal narrative'. As Libby Purves comments:

> We think that we need to see the heart that beats beneath every suit and motivates every action, though only the action itself affects us. (*The Times*, 30 August 2010)

So the Oxford-educated Tony Blair used glottal stops to portray himself as an 'ordinary bloke' and football fan; the preppy George W. Bush set up an image as a Texan son of the soil and David Cameron, the wealthy, Eton-educated, British Prime Minister, has photos taken of him doing the washing up in his kitchen so that we may see him as an 'ordinary family man'.

In a politics of bullshit, 'facts' are just boring and/or irrelevant. Instead, policy is made on the basis of focus groups and perceptions. As Tony Blair said in 2006, policymaking on law and order 'is not about statistics, it is about how people feel ... the fear of crime is as important in some respects as crime itself' (quoted in *The Economist*, 24 June 2006).

Let me offer you a few examples of what I mean. In the summer of 2005, the British Financial Services Authority (FSA) was reported as reacting furiously to comments by Tony Blair that 'the UK's financial regulator is seen as strangling respectable businesses'. A spokeswoman defended Blair's speech saying:

> The prime minister of course values the work of the FSA but he was talking about *people's perceptions*. If parents, members of the public and business *perceive* that there is too much red tape and regulation in their day-to-day lives, it is right that the government looks at this. (*Guardian*, 6 June 2005, my emphasis)

Similarly, recent British governments maintain, against the scientific evidence, a failed policy of banning 'soft' drugs because they are worried about how legislation will be perceived. As John Tatam puts it:

> The government has indeed sent out a clear message to young people: it is not interested in the facts about the relative harm of drugs, only 'public perceptions'. (*Guardian*, Letters, 10 May 2008)

We see here governments making policy not in terms of a cool analysis of facts but as a kneejerk response to people's 'perceptions' (which often themselves are little more than the latest newspaper headline). As has happened in the area of drugs, this sets up a vicious circle where changes in the law become more and more out of touch with reality. Such on-the-hoof policymaking is simply bullshit.

My final example is taken from the announcement a few years ago of US plans for a manned mission to Mars. Despite all the evidence that unmanned missions give you far more bangs per buck, this is what I heard a Professor at the California Institute of Technology (Caltech) say on BBC TV World News to support Bush's plans for a manned Mars mission: 'Actually having a human being experience being on Mars is important. That means that millions of people on Earth can experience it too.'

We might contest this justification for manned flights to Mars simply by asking: what does it mean to 'experience' Mars? How can we experience an alien planet except through an Earthly framework, for example, by comparing what we see to what we know about Earth and/or what we have seen in media science fiction like Star Wars or Star Trek? In this sense, the Caltech's professor's appeal to 'experience' is, yet again, bullshit.

In stressing 'experience' in this way, the Caltech professor enables me to make a link with what will be one of my key themes: the prioritisation of the category of (authentic) experience in both contemporary culture and qualitative research. Let me take one relatively inoffensive example of this.

In their recent, generally excellent, book *Criminological Research* (2004), Noaks and Wincup call for better transcription of our data. This is, indeed, a sensible idea. Too often qualitative researchers 'clean up' their transcripts, supporting their arguments with 'extracts' from, say, interviews or focus groups. Such tidied-up extracts fail to report hesitations or pauses or to place the chosen material within a sequence of interactions (see Chapter 3). But this is not Noaks and Wincup's argument for cleaner transcripts. Instead, they suggest that better transcripts 'will communicate more to the reader about the attitude and state of mind of the interviewee' (2004: 130).

In this revealing passage, we see transcripts being viewed as a guide to psychological states. So, when a member of the public speaks to an interviewer or focus group, they are assumed to be simply evoking their pre-existing states of mind and describing their inner states. But, as we saw in Chapter 3, to speak is to engage in various activities. Through such activities, inner states are already available to other participants who understand your words.

For instance, if I ask you 'Are you free next Saturday night?', I bet you anything you like that you will hear it as a preface to an upcoming 'invitation'. If you don't want to accept my invitation (which has not even been offered yet), you will provide an excuse or even just hesitate. I will then understand that I should not offer my invitation and we will have managed to let each other off lightly. So to treat what we say as simply describing our inner states is to take a commonsense point of view which plays what might be called 'the experience game' in the same way as TV chatshow hosts, their guests and audiences.

It is now time to conclude this preamble and to set out my main argument. It will have four main components:

1   Contemporary qualitative research has been infiltrated by two elements: the experience game of romanticism and (as we'll see in a moment) the pastiche of postmodernism.

2 Both these elements derive from an unthinking adoption of certain features of contemporary culture. I will suggest that following this path is dangerous – think of the perverted versions of science in the mid-twentieth century when Soviet science and Nazi science flourished.

3 Under these auspices, qualitative research can amount to 'bullshit' conceived. Not in its pejorative and vernacular sense, but as overly kitsch, overly jargonised and over-theorised.

4 Returning to some themes raised in Chapter 1, I will conclude by suggesting an alternative aesthetic for qualitative research (more counter-culture than culture).

Unfortunately, arguments like these may be fighting a losing battle. To the extent that qualitative researchers have largely embraced contemporary culture, their work is largely bullshit.

This presupposes a number of issues. First, how are we to characterise contemporary qualitative research? On the basis of sales alone, the three editions of the *Handbook of Qualitative Research* edited by Norman Denzin and Yvonna Lincoln have an iconic character. How do these scholars define our field? In their editorials, they describe what they call two 'common research styles' in qualitative research. I have set these out below with explanatory comments by the authors:

- *Capturing the individual's point of view*

    Qualitative investigators think they can get closer to the actor's perspective through detailed interviewing and observation. They argue that quantitative researchers are seldom able to capture their subjects' perspectives.

- *Acceptance of postmodern sensibilities*

    Alternative methods ... including emotionality, personal responsibility, an ethic of caring, political praxis, multivoiced texts, and dialogues with subjects. (Denzin and Lincoln, 2000: 10)

I believe that Denzin and Lincoln have brilliantly grasped two concerns which animate a great deal of contemporary qualitative research. I also agree with their argument, voiced elsewhere in their writings, that research does not exist in a vacuum but is intimately tied to the workings of modern society.

In what follows, I will look at each 'style' in turn, emphasizing the way in which each links to taken-for-granted aspects of contemporary culture. In doing so, I will attempt to separate 'is' and 'ought' questions. If we accept Denzin and Lincoln's diagnosis of the concerns of qualitative research, should we embrace it?

▬▬▬ Experience and our cultural love affair with the 'real'

Denzin and Lincoln's portrayal of what qualitative researchers 'think they can [do]' (first quotation) appears to differentiate us beautifully from those benighted number-crunchers whose concern for mere 'facts' precludes a proper understanding of what Denzin and Lincoln call 'the actor's perspective'. According to this view, our research concerns itself with '[the] perspectives of the participants and their diversity' (Flick, 1998: 27) and attempts 'to document the world from the point of view of the people studied' (Hammersley, 1992: 165). Or, as Laura Sheard describes the design of her study of women in the night-time economy:

> This study uses qualitative methodology through employment of the in-depth, semi-structured interview. Qualitative research places importance on understanding the social world through the perceptions, attitudes and experiences of individuals. In-depth interviews represent one of the best possible ways in which to access … experiences, thoughts and opinions. (2011: 623)

This attention to the 'perspective', 'point of view' and 'experiences' of the people we study reveals a rarely challenged consensus about the nature of our enterprise and its analytical targets. Although, as Flick points out (1998: 17), it is often associated with the symbolic interactionist tradition, it extends itself much more generally throughout qualitative research.

Yet what such researchers call 'the actor's perspective' is a very slippery notion as their intellectual ancestor, Max Weber (1949), was well aware. As Weber pointed out nearly a century ago, there is no one-to-one relationship between our understandings and our actions. Indeed, given the routinised nature of much behaviour, isn't it dangerous to assume that there is a 'point of view' or 'perspective' lying behind every act?

There is a further problem. Most qualitative researchers who champion the subject's point of view or privilege experience simply do not question where the subject's 'viewpoint' comes from or how 'experience' gets defined the way it does by those very individuals whose experience they seek to document. Don't these emerge, in some way or other, from the varied contexts out of which we 'draw from experience' to convey accounts of who and what we are?

A telling example is provided in an anecdote about one of Jay Gubrium's doctoral students (Gubrium and Holstein, 2002: 21–2). The student interviewed pharmacists who had engaged in substance abuse. His aim was to understand how those who 'should know better' accounted for what had happened to them. As it turned out, what these pharmacists said closely fitted the familiar recovery rubrics of self-help groups. Indeed, many had attended groups like Alcoholics Anonymous (AA) and Narcotics Anonymous (NA). So in what sense were these accounts the pharmacists 'own' stories? As Gubrium pointed out, don't these stories 'belong' not only to individuals but to particular organisational discourses which are merely 'voiced' here?

Of course, Gubrium's observation is foreign to how the mass media depict our lives. These claim to offer 'authentic experience' by looking deep inside our innermost thoughts and feelings. As the journalist Ludovic Hunter-Tilney has suggested, there is a ready market for such bullshit: 'The market for true-life experience is large and often profitable, whether manifested in voyeuristic reality television or painstaking dramatic reconstructions of real events' (*Financial Times*, 2003).

It seems that the media go beyond looking for 'authentic' emotions; they *demand* them. For instance, grieving relatives and friends should properly cry. Take the example given in Box 5.3.

Box 5.3   Murder in the outback

In 2004–5, British and Australian newspapers were running a big story about a British backpacker, Joanne Lees, who narrowly escaped from a roadside attack in the Australian outback during which her boyfriend was murdered. It turns out that, despite her horrific experience, her character was pilloried by the media shortly afterwards. The main reason given was that her account of what happened was strangely 'unemotional'. At the trial of her alleged attacker, she is now showing that she has learned her 'mistake'. This time round, the prosecution counsel has asked her several questions about how she felt at the time and Lees is reported to have given very emotional answers, even breaking down in tears.

Where are Lees's emotions? Are they outpourings of how she felt at the time or right now? Or is Lees cooperating with the lawyer in producing a display of emotion appropriate to her situation? And isn't this how emotions usually work? For instance, Heath (1986) shows how a cry of 'pain' in a medical consultation is closely tied to the interaction between doctor and patient – it does not recur when a 'painful' part of the body is touched by the doctor a second time.

As the Lees case illustrates, TV news programmes and documentaries increasingly cater to our demand to get inside people's heads and to see 'raw' emotion. Take the example below, garnered more or less at random:

> Mother 'relieved' at son's release from Camp X-Ray (BBC TV tele-text headline)

You might say 'How on earth can a mother be anything other than relieved by her son's release from internment? Surely, it would only be newsworthy if such a mother wanted her son to stay in Camp X-Ray and was upset by his release?'

Yet our media (and, to be fair, most of us) demand such snippets of apparently 'lived experience'. The fact that they turn out to be entirely predictable seems to be of no account. Indeed, it is demanded of us all that we should have the appropriate emotional response. Think, for instance, how successful athletes so often tell interviewers that 'it has not sunk in yet'. After all, they need to be seen like we perceive ourselves, as decent people, surprised by good fortune.

Rarely does the absurdity of these kind of responses sink in. For instance, after the rescue of some men from a recent mine disaster in the US, a TV interviewer asked a mine official:

Interviewer: How did people feel after the men were released?
Official: Actually I was too busy talking to people like you. (US TV report)

This is a rare example of an interviewee refusing to play 'the experience game'. The mine official shows us that this kind of discourse of 'feelings' is a product of media demands. Occasions like mine accidents and murders (particularly of children) are marvellous grist to the media mill. Referring to the reporting of the immediate aftermath to the murder in Soham, England, of two young girls, a critic wrote:

> How do you feel about the abduction and murder of those two ten-year-old girls? Come on, how do you really feel? Yes, you're right, it's a crassly stupid, pointless and insensitive question. So why have much of the media spent the past fortnight demanding answers to that and similar questions from everybody in Soham and beyond? ('These mawkish tears are an insult', *The Times*, Mick Hume, 19 August 2002)

As Mick Hume shows, contemporary reporting both depicts 'raw' emotion and demands that all of us should feel strong emotions about an event irrespective of whether we have any personal connection with it. Increasingly, the media succeeds – think of the millions around the world who wept at the death of Princess Diana despite a 'relationship' with her limited to fleeting images on a screen. Or think of how we feel compelled to express our grief in public.

Take this blog on LiveJournal which I mentioned in Chapter 1:

> *36-year-old male*: I wish i had the magic to give Janine the life i stole from her. of all the people i've hurt in my life, it's her that i feel most dreadful about. she put so much trust and faith in me ... and i really loved her. i still do. yet i screwed her over and tore that wonderful heart in two. if only i had some way to make it so i'd never happened to her life ... if i could just patch up my era [*sic*] with a big sander bandaid ... so that it had been him that she'd met and not me. admittedly, i'd lose a part of my life that means a lot to me ... but i'd really rather never to have hurt her. and no matter how sorry i am, and how deeply i feel the grief, the apologies i give her can never unhurt her. (Hookway, 2008: 102–3).

As Ludovic Hunter-Tilney comments about such public displays of grief: 'The new generation of memoirists don't bother to alter the details of their lives. They invite us to feel their pain' (*Financial Times*, 12 March 2005).

In the modern world, we see what Frances Stonor Saunders calls 'an appetite for grief' (2011: 2). So we assume that 'whatever the problem, it is better to talk about it' (Porter, 1995: 15). And modern politicians recognise how we have come to see what was once private grief as a public matter. Think of Tony Blair's tearful description of Diana as 'the people's princess'. Failing to pay attention to 'authentic' emotions is a sure route to political death, as Patricia Hewitt, a UK cabinet minister suggested: 'politicians have lost trust due to ... a society that places a premium on the authenticity of personal experience' (*Guardian*, 23 June 2005).

As Hewitt observes, one inescapable fact about the cultural milieu of the Western World is that 'lived experience' must be pursued and interrogated. An aspect of this is seen in the work of the 'psy' professions, notably in the methods of the skilled counsellor (see Peräkylä, 1995). Of course, not everybody visits a counsellor or psychiatrist. But many of us avidly watch 'reality' TV shows, soaps and chat shows in which people's 'experience' is very much the target (see Atkinson and Silverman, 1997). And we interact furiously as 'everyone juggles technologies: iPods and Facebook, Blackberrys and landlines' (Bunting, 2010: 29). As Bunting points out, 'the problem is the quality of this connectivity and its potential for addiction – how it is designed to draw people ever deeper' (2010: 29).

Now consider researchers who are tempted by the lure of 'experience'. Put at its starkest, must qualitative research privilege 'experience' and 'feelings' when, in so doing, it is responding to much the same imperatives as a blog, soap opera or therapy session?

As we saw in Chapter 2, although some researchers observe and/or record interactions, the predominant technology of qualitative research is the interview. If you doubt this, look at the attention given to the interview in methodology texts. When qualitative researchers justify using interviews, they tend to forget other qualitative methods and simply stress the advantages of the open-ended interview compared to the quantitative fixed choice interview or questionnaire. For instance, Bridget Byrne suggests that

> qualitative interviewing is particularly useful as a research method for accessing individuals' attitudes and values – things that cannot necessarily be observed or accommodated in a formal questionnaire. Open-ended and flexible questions are likely to get a more considered response than closed questions and therefore provide better access to interviewees' views, interpretation of events, understandings, experiences and opinions ... [qualitative interviewing] *when done well* is able to achieve a level of depth and complexity that is not available to other, particularly survey-based, approaches. (2004: 182, my emphasis)

In order to achieve 'rich data' in the open-ended interview, we are told that the keynote is 'active listening' in which the interviewer 'allows the interviewee the freedom to talk and ascribe meanings' while bearing in mind the broader aims of the project (Noaks and Wincup, 2004: 80). Doesn't this largely replicate the media's use of the interview for constructing the 'immediate' and 'authentic'?

Think of interviews as a modern form of self-understanding. Indeed, a worthwhile task for qualitative researchers would be a comparison of transcripts of interviews with letters and diaries in the eighteenth century and songs and folktales in still earlier eras.

Why might the contemporary novelist Milan Kundera comment that, in democratic societies, it is the interviewer rather than the secret policeman to whom we are answerable (*Immortality*: 123–4)? What does the interview society require?

First, for interviews to work, we must think of ourselves as discrete individuals with personal experiences and goals. This emergence of the self as a proper object of narration may be a relatively modern phenomenon. For instance, in feudal or aristocratic societies, one was primarily identified through membership of a collectivity (e.g. peasant, aristocrat etc.).

Second, the interview demands subjects who are happy to confess their innermost thoughts and emotions to the appropriate professional. Today, the professional who receives their confession is no longer usually a priest but a therapist or media interviewer.

Third, the interview society requires mass-media technologies and myths which give a new twist to the, no doubt, perennial polarities of the private and the public; the routine and the sensational. Judging by the bereaved family members who regularly appear on our TV screens, such technologies and myths generate subjects who are not only happy to confess but seem to feel that their once-private emotions are somehow validated when revealed to a media interviewer.

If we recognise the impact of these historical and cultural changes, it becomes difficult to continue the present situation where qualitative researchers use the interview as an unquestioned resource to look into people's 'experiences'. As Gubrium observed with his pharmacists, when people 'confess' to them, researchers should properly dismiss appeals to the 'immediacy' and 'authenticity' of their data. Instead, they should treat what they hear as simply a contingent narrative or account and examine the cultural resources that speakers skilfully deploy.

I have tried to illustrate the complexities involved when we, as researchers, try to 'capture the individual's point of view'. Let me now turn to the other strand of Denzin and Lincoln's two 'themes': the appeal by qualitative researchers to 'postmodern sensibilities'.

A postmodern world?

It is difficult to deny that, compared to our grandparents, today we live in cultures which are much more fragmented and dislocated. The communal experience of the Internet may have led to the fragmentation of identity, and cyberculture can encourage multiple, fragmented selves (Kozinets, 2010: 37). Annette Markham cautions us that this may be a matter of degree rather an absolute change. Nonetheless, she adds, 'the extent to which our identities are saturated with media, networked with others, and intermingled with information and communication technologies is a recent phenomenon, one worthy of study and reflection' (2011: 121).

In such a postmodern world, 'there is no essence [and] we're moving through a world of signs and wonders, where everything is lying around as cultural wreckage, waiting to be reused, combined in new and unusual ways' (Kunzru, 2011: 18). Within such a world, there is no longer any progress, only oscillation. As Kundera tells us:

> The word *change*, so dear to our old Europe, has been given a new meaning: it no longer means *a new stage of coherent development* (as it was understood by Vico, Hegel or Marx), but a *shift from one side to another*, from front to back, from the back to the left, from the left to the front (as understood by designers dreaming up the fashion for the next season). (1989: 129)

So, Kundera tells us, in the (post-) modern world, Karl Marx's concept of ruling ideas ('ideology') has been replaced by *imagology*, in which master narratives are replaced by pastiche (1989: 127). In this context, Puccini's operatic aria 'Nessun Dorma' becomes permanently linked to the Football World Cup. And Michael Jackson replaces Lenin in Bucharest:

> A Michael Jackson cardboard cut-out struts on a Bucharest plinth once occupied by a statue of Lenin, to advertise the star's first appearance in Romania. (caption beneath a photograph, *The Times*, 3 October 1992)

The power of imagology was summed up after the fall of Communism by New Year's Eve 1992 when the only red flag in Moscow was reported by BBC radio to be outside McDonald's! All of this seems to support the view of Paul, a character in Kundera's novel *Immortality*, who predicts:

> Things will lose ninety per cent of their meaning and will become light. In such a weightless environment, fanaticism will disappear. War will become impossible. (Kundera, 2000: 135)

Paul's predictions look like the post-Soviet New World Order or what Francis Fukuyama (2010) has called 'the end of history'. In this new world order, irony, resistance and subversion are already incorporated into imagology. Think of a David Lynch movie or *The Simpsons* cartoon. Or consider the play of images in modern advertising.

For instance, at the time of the collapse of the Soviet Empire, in 1992, the British company Vodafone ran an advert headed 'The Mobile Phone Revolution'. It depicted a woman who is wearing something like a Red Army uniform. She has adopted a revolutionary posture. In the accompanying text, the words 'October' and 'Revolution' are linked to Vodafone's products.

Kundera reminds us that we live in a *postmodern* world in which identity is reduced to a play of images. In this shift, the romantic appeal to a stable self is unsettled:

> It's naive to believe that our image is only an illusion that conceals our selves, as the only true essence independent of the eyes of the world. The imagologues have revealed with cynical radicalism that the reverse is true: our self is a mere illusion, ungraspable, indescribable, misty, while the only reality, all too easily graspable and describable, is our image in the eyes of others. And the worst thing about it is that you are not its master. (2000: 143)

A contemporary example of how our identities seem to be created through images is the iconic reality TV show *Big Brother*. In the commentary that follows, Michael Bywater nicely sketches the ironic selves displayed in this programme.

- The contestants are pretending to be ordinary people, though of course
- They cannot be ordinary people because they are now on TV but
- They were ordinary people before they went on TV which means that
- They are even more extraordinary than they would be if they weren't ordinary people but actors, because, after all,
- It is a really, really extraordinary thing for ordinary people to be on TV which is why
- They then get invited to host their own chat shows or write their own books. (2006: 118)

If we follow Bywater and assume that reality TV is 'just playing at Wendy House, or rather watching people playing at Wendy House' (2006: 118), then, like Kundera, we have entered a world in which 'our self is a mere illusion'. This postmodern situation seems totally to negate the essentially romantic pursuit of 'inner experience'. However, there are reasons to doubt some of Kundera's diagnosis.

First, how many ordinary people feel that their self is, as Kundera argues, 'a mere illusion'? Don't we cling to our own sense of our 'identity'? And doesn't the interview society trade off this very assumption?

Second, postmodern arguments about the instability of the self look a little odd when we examine the stories that contemporary people tell about themselves. From the sad blogger to the tragic tales of bereaved family members and Gubrium's substance-abusing pharmacists, we see people with a clear sense of their identities using quite stable narrative formats (from the blogger's 'confession' to 'the heroic victim' and 'the recovery rubric' of self-help groups).

All this suggests that our postmodern world has incorporated rather than overturned the romantic themes that probably originated in the nineteenth-century. This reveals that contemporary culture contains both romantic and postmodern themes. However, does this mean that qualitative research must model such a world?

▦ Postmodern research?

> The world of signs is fast, liquid, delirious, disposable. Clever people approach it with scepticism. Sincerity is out. Irony is in. And style. (Kunzru, 2011: 18).

What Denzin and Lincoln call 'postmodern sensibilities' has, in some quarters, become identified with cutting-edge research. Judging by the calls for papers at recent conferences, 'qualitative research' now encompasses such postmodern approaches as 'performance ethnography', 'ethnodrama' and poetry.

While the first two topics may be pretty opaque to most readers, we all think we know what poetry is and might wonder why it is now appearing at conferences concerned with qualitative research. The example in Box 5.4 may help. It is the abstract of a journal article entitled 'The research poem in international social work: Innovations in qualitative methodology'.

Box 5.4   Poetry as qualitative research

Postmodern researchers have recognized the value of studying the lived, subjective experience of individuals and groups. Less concerned with statistical generalizability, such authors instead are interested in 'metaphoric generalizability,' the degree to which qualitative data penetrate the essence of human experience and reveal themselves fully to an engaged audience. The goal of such generating and presenting of this type of data is to inspire an empathic, emotional reaction, so the consumer of research can develop a deep, personal understanding of the 'subject' of the data. (Furman et al., 2006)

This abstract is a marvellous blend of postmodern verbiage (what on earth is 'metaphoric generalizability'?) combined with an appeal to the whole gamut of romantic concepts including 'empathy', 'emotion' and 'deep, personal understanding'. The reasoning behind it is well captured in the authors' statement that

> traditional qualitative data, such as in-depth interviews or ethnographic reports ... are often too impersonal or dense to be easily consumed and often leave readers overwhelmed or unmoved. [Instead] we explore the uses of poetry and poetic structures and forms as valuable tools of qualitative social research. Based on practices from expressive arts research and more traditional qualitative methods, the research poem can present evocative, powerful insights that can teach us about the lived experience of social work clients. (Furman et al., 2006: 1)

In such a romantic pursuit of 'lived experience', it becomes acceptable to abandon standard qualitative research methods (now dubbed 'traditional') which apparently leave readers 'overwhelmed or unmoved'. Furman et al. now invent something they call 'the research poem' – a concept which has me baffled just as much as their idea of 'metaphoric generalizability'.

As qualitative research defines itself less and less in terms of 'science' and more in terms of an 'artistic' performance, drama as well as poetry has become an acceptable research tool – as exemplified in the journal abstract given in Box 5.5.

Box 5.5   Dramatising women's stories

This paper focuses upon renewed methodologies for social research in order to explore and re-present the complexity of lived relations in contemporary society. Renewed methodologies can transgress conventional or traditional ways of analysing and representing research data. This paper combines socio-cultural theory; experience (life stories); and practice (exhibition/performance) defined as ethno-mimesis to explore and better understand key themes and issues evolving from ethnographic work with female prostitutes. By focusing upon life history work with women working as prostitutes and by experiencing women's stories represented through live art we can further our understanding of the complexity of sex, sexualities, desire, violence, masculinities and the relevance of the body. (O'Neill, 2002)

As anybody who has been to the theatre can testify, what O'Neill calls 'live art' can fascinate and grip us. However, conceived as 'research', 'live art' has a problem, since the concepts of 'truth' and even 'accuracy' take on a very different meaning in art as compared to research. So 'ethnomimesis' (or 'ethnodrama' as it often called) can be artistically gripping but factually inaccurate.

Take the following review of another ethnodrama, this time about illegal drug use. The reviewer, Mercer Sullivan, finds some merit in the work but adds the following comment:

> I write as a professional ethnographer who conducted direct studies of drug dealers and users in New York City in the early and mid-1980's, up through the beginning of the crack epidemic. Since then, I have continued to study other aspects of inner-city life, all of them profoundly influenced by crack, and I have worked with other ethnographers who have studied crack users and dealers. [Despite the merits of the article] there are a number of inaccuracies; a more serious problem is that the image projected by the ethnodrama is tied to a particular kind of speaker and place, with no acknowledgement of this fact. The inaccuracies concern the pharmacology and history of smokable cocaine. (Sullivan, 1993)

Writing as an ethnographer who has researched drug use, Sullivan thus makes two crucial criticisms of the article. First, he finds simple factual errors. Second, he notes that the speakers represented in an ethnodrama can only tell us part of the story.

This is hardly surprising. Poetry and 'ethnodrama' inhabit a very different world to those worlds (including scientific research as well as courts of law) whose business is making factual claims and where, consequently, some version of 'evidence' matters. Once you discount an appeal to evidence, anything goes (including poetry and ethnodrama).

The problem that this generates has been well stated by Alain Sokal and Jean Bricmont's definition of postmodernism as:

> An intellectual current characterised by the more-or-less explicit rejection of the rationalist tradition of the Enlightenment, by theoretical discourses disconnected from any empirical test (and) a cognitive and cultural relativism that regards science as nothing more than a 'narration', a 'myth' or a social construction among many others. (1998: 1)

Sokal and Bricmont's book started as an elaborate joke based on a spoof article which Sokal submitted to an academic journal called *Social Text*.

The article had the highfalutin' title 'Transgressing the boundaries: Towards a transformative hermeneutics of quantum gravity'. The article was accepted and published in a special issue devoted to rebutting the criticisms levelled against postmodernism. Box 5.6 illustrates how they describe what the article said.

Box 5.6   A postmodern spoof

The article 'is brimming with absurdities and blatant non sequiturs.' In addition, it asserts an extreme form of cognitive relativism: after mocking the old-fashioned 'dogma' that 'there exists an external world, whose properties are independent of any human being and indeed of humanity as a whole', it proclaims categorically that 'physical reality', no less than 'social reality', is at bottom a social and linguistic construction. (Sokal and Bricmont, 1998: 1–2)

As Sokal and Bricmont tell us, by unwittingly publishing this spoof, the editors of the journal had found a spectacular way to shoot themselves in the foot. One reviewer of the book commented:

> This book will be a purgatory for those oppressed by pseudo-scientific sociology or the scorn of the French avant-garde. And it gives an entertaining insight into the weird notions that apparently intelligent people may hold.

Consider this example from (the postmodern feminist) Irigay:" 'Is e=mc² a sexed equation? Let us make the hypothesis that it is insofar as it privileges the speed of light over other speeds that are vitally necessary to us'. There is, of course, an alternative hypothesis: that 'Irigay has not the faintest idea of what she is trying to say' (Max Wilkinson, *Financial Times Weekend*, 18–19 July 1998).

This episode illustrates the way in which self-proclaimed 'postmodern research' can willingly lose contact with claims based on evidence and couched in propositional language. Dressed up in doubtful theoretical verbiage, it not only advocates that 'anything goes' but actually prefers 'ethnodrama, story [and] poetry' to clear, refutable statements about research findings.

In this respect, academic postmodernism bears frightening resemblances to the way arrogant politicians believe they can deny reality by creating their own 'facts'. In a discussion of Donald Rumsfeld's attempt to redefine what has happened in Iraq since the invasion, the journalist Oliver Burkeman has come up with an intriguing example of such fact-creation. He writes:

> In 2004, an unnamed White House official told the journalist Ron Suskind, disparagingly, that critics like Suskind inhabited the 'reality-based community ... We're an empire now, and when we act, we create our own reality.' (*Guardian*, 10 November 2006)

However, just because we live in what is, in politics and elsewhere, a postmodern world, does not mean that all our endeavours must, willingly or unwillingly, defer to its themes of dislocation and decentring. In academia, if we ignore reality and actively encourage experimental and self-referential writing, we end up reducing all literature (literary and scientific) to solipsism. As Hunter-Tilney has observed, such trends suggest

> the alarming possibility that the only experience [the writer] will be left to write about is his writing ... an end state of pure solipsism: entirely self-referential, nothing in [the writing] will be real other than the writer and his words. (*Financial Times*, 2003)

Franz Kafka's short story 'Investigations of a Dog' (1961) (published in his *Metamorphosis and Other Stories*, 1961) creates a marvellous image of 'airdogs' (*Lufthunde*) who, like the postmodern intellectuals that Sokal and Bricmont satirise, get above themselves. However, in Kafka's story, this is a literary transcendance – his airdogs float on cushions above the ground, surveying the world from on high, yet cut off from any contact with it. Indeed, they are so cut off that Kafka's doggy narrator wonders how they manage to reproduce themselves!

Kafka's airdogs, like good bullshitters, seek to make grand statements but end up by getting above themselves. However, so far I have simply been giving illustrations of what 'bullshit' is. Without pushing the metaphor too far, it is now time to get deeper down among the bullshit. In doing so, I will draw upon a marvellous book by the American philosopher Harry G. Frankfurt (2005). This book was called simply *On Bullshit* and was the inspiration for this chapter.

On Bullshit

Frankfurt begins his short book by observing that 'one of the most salient features of our culture is that there is so much bullshit' (2005: 1). He points out that the realms of advertising and of public relations, and the nowadays closely related realm of politics, are replete with instances of bullshit.

Think once more of Prime Minister Blair's depiction of Princess Diana as 'the people's princess'. We do not need to suggest that Blair did not believe what he was saying. As Frankfurt argues, 'The bullshitter may not deceive, or even intend to do so, either about the facts or about what he takes the facts to be' (2005: 55). Why, then, was Blair's image bullshit? Deception is at the heart of the matter. The bullshitter 'attempts to deceive us about his enterprise ... he misrepresents what he is up to' (2005: 54). Unlike the liar, who wants us to believe something that he knows to be false, the bullshitter conceals something different. As Frankfurt puts it:

> The fact about himself that the bullshitter hides ... is that the truth value of his statements are of no central interest to him ... the motive guiding and controlling [his speech] is unconcerned with how the things about which he speaks truly are ... He does not care whether the things he says describe reality correctly. He just picks them out, or makes them up, to suit his purpose. (2005: 55–6)

As we have seen, in the (post)modern world, many fields of enterprise depend upon such indifference to the truth. For instance, Benson and Stangroom specify in this group 'advertising, PR, fashion, lobbying, marketing [and] entertainment'. As they point out,

> there are whole large, well-paid, high-status sectors of the economy where truth–scepticism, wishful thinking, fantasy, suspension of disbelief, deletion of the boundary between dreams and reality, are not only not a handicap but essential to the enterprise. Much of capitalism rests on peddling illusions and fantasies, and most of the entertainment industry would be lost without them. (2006: 164)

The question is: should qualitative research happily peddle such 'illusions and fantasies'? Think back to the article published by *Social Text*. Sokal and Bricmont had undoubtedly produced a piece of bullshit. Unconcerned by truth, they had picked out and made up statements to suit their purpose. More important, for my present purposes, the editors of this journal had published their paper without, apparently, checking whether its statements were true. The paper suited their (postmodern) purposes and so they published it. In Frankfurt's sense, their decision was 'bullshit'.

However, Frankfurt goes beyond diagnosing the problem. He wants to help us to understand its historical and cultural roots. As he asks, 'Why is there so much bullshit?' (2005: 62). He notes that bullshit is unavoidable when people are required to talk about things about which they know little. Think of what I have called 'the interview society'. The broadcast media and various polling organisations routinely use interviews with ordinary people to produce what TV news stations call 'vox pop' (the voice of the people) on every subject under the sun. As Frankfurt puts it, contemporary culture exhibits 'the widespread conviction that it is the responsibility of a citizen in a democracy to have opinions about everything' (2005: 63–4).

Yet the spread of bullshit extends well beyond the confines of popular culture. Indeed, Frankfurt argues that intellectuals have been complicit in this process.

The Sokal and Bricmont incident reveals the way in which the truth-value of statements seems no longer to concern journal editors. Underlying this position is a postmodern framework of thought which has generated 'various forms of skepticism which deny that we can have any reliable access to an objective reality, and which therefore reject the possibility of knowing how things are' (Frankfurt, 2005: 64). Such 'anti-realist' doctrines 'undermine confidence in the value of disinterested efforts to determine what is true and what is false, and even in the intelligibility of the notion of objective inquiry' (2005: 65).

Frankfurt's depiction of a crisis of confidence in 'objective inquiry' is underlined if we return to my earlier discussion of the equation of poetry and ethnodrama with qualitative research. While each of these traditions may have worthwhile ends, many of their proponents seem, at best, ambiguous about what Frankfurt calls 'the value of disinterested efforts to determine what is true and what is false' (2005: 65).

Moreover, because 'objective inquiry' is no longer the name of the (postmodern) game, it follows that 'anything goes' becomes the motto for how we communicate. No longer do we want sober papers which dress themselves in the clothes of a now discredited 'science'. Instead, ethnodrama and poetry are to be valued because they 'inspire an empathic, emotional reaction' unlike more conventional approaches which allegedly leave readers 'overwhelmed and unmoved' (Furman et al., 2006: 1).

So standard ideas about how we reason are being rethought and replaced by something that its proponents call 'radical thought'. In an era of what Benson and Stangroom call 'epistemic relativism',

> the underlying idea in the rethinking process is that radical thought can go anywhere and tackle anything: that the rethinking is inherently and necessarily political, not factual or technical; that it is a matter of morals, of value, of justice, rather than one of statistics; of ought rather than is. This implies both that anyone and everyone is qualified to engage in it, and that no one is qualified to gainsay its insights on the basis of expertise or technical knowledge. (2006: 45)

This version links postmodern scholars with the kind of Blairite policy-making based on 'people's perceptions' that I discussed earlier in this chapter. These postmodern fashions in the academy may appear as an advance over fuddyduddy ways. In my view, however, they represent a retreat. Presenting our work as poetry involves:

> A retreat from the discipline required by a dedication to the ideal of *correctness* to a quite different sort of discipline which is imposed by pursuit of an alternative ideal of *sincerity*. Rather than seeking primarily to arrive at accurate representations of a common world, the individual turns toward trying to provide honest representations of himself. (Frankfurt, 2005: 65)

I have nothing in principle against these ways of expressing yourself. There are many examples of, for instance, poetry and even cartoons being used as powerful critiques of political institutions. But think about what follows if poetry or cartoons become more important than the propositional language of scientific discourse. Where does this leave researchers struggling to get a sound grasp of their data? Just as seriously, where does it leave the standing of our writing in the public eye? Who is going to fund research or to implement research findings if we communicate via ethnodrama or poetry?

Moreover, the appeal to 'sincerity' in writing is ultimately misplaced. Once again, Frankfurt makes the point that 'there is nothing in theory, and certainly nothing in experience to support the extraordinary judgment that ... the truth about himself ... is the easiest for a person to know. Our natures are elusively insubstantial – notoriously less stable and less inherent than the natures of other things. And insofar as this is the case, *sincerity is bullshit*' (2005: 67, my emphasis).

Following Frankfurt, the experimental writing, sometimes including poetry, that increasingly populates some academic journals is, strictly speaking, bullshit. But what is the alternative to bullshit?

It is time to lay all my cards on the table. You will not be surprised to see that I differ from the postmodernists in my sense of 'critical enquiry'. For them, being 'critical' involves overturning every standard that has governed enquiry since the Enlightenment sought to replace blinkered faith-based thought in the eighteenth century. For me, being 'critical' involves simply doing your best to separate 'fact' from 'fancy' and writing as clearly as possible to allow your readers properly to weigh up your arguments.

This is quite a 'traditional' programme in the sense that it draws upon the conventional wisdom of most Western scientific thought in the twentieth century. Let us look a bit more closely at what it involves.

▆▆▆▆ An anti-bullshit agenda for qualitative research

In this part of the chapter, I will briefly outline some standards to which social science researchers might properly aspire. I refer to 'aspirations' because I am not claiming that any piece of research can be straightforwardly 'determined' by any principle. Instead, we are dealing here with features that qualitative researchers can keep at the back of their minds and the readers of their work can use to judge them.

None of this is revolutionary stuff. Indeed, in the present intellectual climate, it may be regarded as counter-revolutionary. For most of the ideas and ideals set out below have been around for centuries, indeed millenia.

▆▆▆ Clarity

Earlier in this chapter, we encountered an architecture student who thought she had to dress up her research project in overblown, theoretical language. As opposed to this 'peacock's tail syndrome', I suggest that one's bias, wherever possible, should be in favour of plain, clear language.

The mid-twentieth century philosopher of science Karl Popper was a major proponent of this view and, consequently, the scourge of jargon-ridden writing. Even in his day, when postmodernism was hardly conceived, Popper recognised that this was no easy task. As he put it,

> one has to train oneself constantly to write and to speak in a clear and simple language. Every thought should be formulated as clearly and simply as possible.

> This can only be achieved by hard work. (Popper, 1976: 292)

▆▆▆ Reason

Given the radical critique of the claims of scientific method made by postmodernists, we need to remind ourselves of one simple fact. As Popper has argued, science is not about unrealistic, rigid principles. Nor does it frown upon unorthodoxy. Rather science simply demands that, as you examine your data, you give your best shot to being self-critical, cautious and avoiding jumping to conclusions. In short, you should attempt to be 'reasonable'. In this sense, as Sokal and Bricmont note,

the scientific method is not radically different from the rational attitude in everyday life ... Historians, detectives and plumbers ... use the
same basic methods of induction, deduction and assessment of
evidence. (1998: 54)

Economy

This looks like an odd standard for qualitative research. Ordinarily, we
might locate this term within the science of economics – a notably 'hard',
quantitative social science. However, here I am using the term as in the
phrase 'economy of effort', meaning no more than is required.

To talk about 'economy' in this sense means that we should properly
expect our accounts and explanations to use the minimum of conceptual
tools. So, if one concept or theory will do, we should not use more. This
means of avoiding 'the peacock's tail syndrome' was propounded centuries ago in the principle known as 'Occam's razor': it means that we
should slice away at our explanations till they are down to the very
minimum necessary to account for our data.

Beauty

'Beauty' may seem like a strange aesthetic ideal in a chapter that values
scientific method. However, as theoretical physicists tell us, it turns out
that the most long-lasting accounts of the universe are not only relatively
simple but are also aesthetically pleasing.

It is not inappropriate to ask similar questions about scientific
accounts in our own field. For instance, is the account beautiful? Does
it resolve disputes by rearranging the existing pieces in a pleasing way
or by introducing a new piece which discloses a previously invisible
order?

Truth

A concern for the aesthetic standard of 'beauty' in our accounts might
seem to set us back among the postmodernists. Yet, as one of the most
quoted texts on postmodern anthropology argues, 'to recognize the
poetic dimensions of ethnography does not require that one give up facts
and accurate accounting for the supposed free play of poetry' (Clifford
and Marcus, 1986: 26).

As Clifford and Marcus recognise, a concern for beauty in our accounts must never 'give up' on 'the facts'. Almost half a century ago, the philosopher of science Michael Polyani put it this way:

> No scientific theory is beautiful if it is false and no invention is truly ingenious if it is impracticable ... The standards of scientific value and of inventive ingenuity must still be satisfied. (1964: 195)

What Polyani calls 'the standards of scientific value' also means that, while we need theories and concepts to stimulate our understandings, the facts must remain paramount. The ethnographer Howard Becker uses the example of the US Census to make this point:

> Recognizing the conceptual shaping of our perceptions, it is still true that not everything our concepts would let us see actually turns up ... If we said that the population of the United States, counted the way the Census counts (e.g. excluding such categories as transgender), consisted of 50% men and 50% women, the Census report could certainly tell us that the story is wrong. We don't accept stories that are not borne out by the facts we have available. (1998: 18)

Using very plain language, Ophelia Benson and Jeremy Stangroom make Becker's point about the difference between 'stories' and facts:

> It's a kind of fraud, setting up as a scholar – as someone who engages in research – while disbelieving in the existence or reality of truth. That thought should apply to any branch of enquiry. It is simply part of the job description, and a very important part at that. Detectives and forensic scientists are supposed to collect evidence in order to find the true perpetrators, not false ones. They are not under orders to plant evidence, or to conceal, tamper with, throw out evidence. The same applies to any other kind of enquiry. Getting things wrong, providing false, incorrect inaccurate answers to questions is not the goal. So people with a programmatic, or perhaps temperamental, disbelief in even the possibility of truth, have no business going into any branch of enquiry or pedagogy at all. (2006: 164)

As Benson and Stangroom suggest, if you have a (postmodern) 'disbelief in even the possibility of truth', there are plenty of fields in the contemporary world where bullshit (i.e. indifference to the truth) is no handicap. Think back to my earlier examples from politics and certain kinds of journalism.

Yet again, the issue is: should our research posture simply mimic trends in contemporary culture? Or should it critically analyse these trends and, where appropriate, take a principled stand against them?

Enough of bullshit. But what about tonsils?

The following is the example I have in mind. It is discussed by Harry Frankfurt and uses a case of tonsillitis to show how far a concern with reason can take you (and also how even such a concern may, in certain contexts, overstep the boundaries of good sense).

Responsibility and truth: Fania Pascal's tonsils

In the following memoir, Pascal recollects an upsetting incident involving her friend, the philosopher Ludwig Wittgenstein:

> I had my tonsils out and was in hospital feeling sorry for myself. Wittgenstein called. I croaked: 'I feel just like a dog that has been run over'. He was disgusted: 'You don't know what a dog that has been run over feels like'. (Pascal, 1984: 28)

It seems that Wittgenstein was disgusted by Pascal's use of an inappropriate metaphor for how she felt. As Frankfurt puts it,

> so far as Wittgenstein can see, Pascal offers a description of a certain state of affairs without genuinely submitting to the constraints which the endeavour to provide an accurate representation of reality imposes. Her fault is not that she fails to get things right, but that she is not even trying ... It is just this lack of connection to a concern with truth – this indifference to how things really are – that I regard as the essence of bullshit. (2005: 32–4)

But is the case of Pascal's tonsils a proper example of bullshit as Frankfurt argues? I don't think so.

What Frankfurt is saying would imply that any use of metaphor in everyday communication is to be avoided. Now, as I have just been arguing, it certainly makes sense to be cautious about using such flowery language in science. However, in everyday life, the demand for 'economical' descriptions simply would not work. As Harvey Sacks has shown, when we interact with each other, we use such formats as proverbs and metaphors to produce desired effects. So, for instance, it can be highly effective to say to one's partner when one is feeling tired while at a social engagement in the wee small hours, 'I'm turning into a pumpkin' (invoking the Cinderella story). The person who doesn't have the skills to use such metaphors (or to recognise their import) may even end up being described as 'autistic'.

So calling Pascal's remarks 'bullshit' turns out to be a 'category error' which, in Wittgenstein's own sense, mistakes the 'language game' of 'science' with that of everyday life. This means that we should be careful about spraying around the charge of 'bullshit'. As the tonsils example shows, scientific reason cannot extend everywhere without threatening the delicacies of everyday life. So 'caution' should be our watchword.

Concluding remarks

I will close on a 'romantic' move beloved by media interviews and some 'psy' professionals and qualitative researchers – a 'confession'. Here is my confession: in a certain sense, this chapter is bullshit. Indeed, the same applies to any textbook.

Successful textbooks employ easy to follow categories and polar oppositions. They 'carve up the field' in a palatable way. Unfortunately, while they may help set you on your way, you will have to unlearn them at some point in your career.

This is because the polarities which you find in textbooks can never completely capture a manifold reality. They may be aids to the sluggish imagination, but no more than that. Nor is one side of a polarity always the 'right side' for you. Ultimately, everything depends on what you yourself are trying to do in your own research project.

So this chapter is 'bullshit' because it works with polarities which can never correspond to the exigencies of the field. Maybe, as the postmodern philosopher Jacques Derrida once suggested, a useful tactic is, as I have done here, to argue for the currently unfashionable side of any polar opposition. This is not to be perverse but to unsettle the assumption that any such polarity can properly describe a complex reality.

My best way to avoid being yet another 'trader in snake oil' is to ask you to be cautious if you are persuaded by anything you have read here. My aim will not have been achieved if you simply accept anything that I have written. Instead, I will be satisfied if you become a little more conscious of the implications of the sometimes unconscious choices you will make on your own research path.

6

A Very Short Conclusion

Textbooks on qualitative research usually set out to cover basic or 'nuts and bolts' questions. They discuss the differences between quantitative and qualitative research and their relevance for particular research problems. They also show you the various kinds of data that we work with and discuss, in a basic way, how we go about analysing them. The more basic texts also walk you through elementary practical issues such as how to find a study population and how to carry out different kinds of interviews.

The aim of this book has been to offer you something quite different. I have tried to provide you with an entry into broader questions that many beginners' textbooks tend to gloss over. For instance, what is the underlying logic of qualitative logic? And what are the key debates about its future direction? In this way, I have sought to give you a taste of the areas of argument that animate real debate in our field among 'insiders'.

While the traditional textbook encourages you to 'dip' into it when you need it, I have tried to write a book that is suitable for reading from cover to cover. If you have done this, you will have noticed, I hope, that it is based on a continuous argument. I have called for research studies that are methodologically inventive, empirically rigorous, theoretically alive but with an eye to practical relevance.

To revert to a textbooky form of speech, this argument can be transformed into a set of five bullet-point 'dos and don'ts' which roughly follow the sequence of preceding chapters. If you want to do valuable qualitative research:

Don't:

- treat everyday life as boring or obvious
- assume that people's experiences are your most reliable source of data and that this always means you need to ask people questions
- think that an adequate research report can be based on quoting a few examples that support your argument
- assume either that qualitative research can offer a direct answer to social problems or that it has nothing practical to offer
- assume that your research needs loads of 'theory' or that it must follow the latest theoretical fashions.

Do:

- treat 'obvious' actions, settings and events as potentially remarkable
- recognise that talk, documents and other artefacts as well as interaction can offer revealing data
- seek to locate what precedes and follows any gobbet of data (look for 'sequences')
- recognise the everyday skills we all use and try to start a dialogue with the people in your study based on understanding how those skills work out in practice
- show that you understand that it is important to develop an argument based on a critical sifting of your data.

This list (and the preceding chapters) are based on the lessons that research practice has taught me. It brings to the fore a number of positions that are implicit in my textbooks. It also attempts, more directly, to convey some of the strategies and 'tricks' (see Becker, 1998) that I have learned through my own long apprenticeship in the trade.

One final thought. In parts of this book, particularly in Chapters 1 and 5, I have sought to distance my project from certain aspects of contemporary culture. In that respect, some of you may have felt that you were dealing with the complaints of a grumpy old man. Well, there is some truth in that depiction. For instance, my wife regularly points out to me that nowadays my reactions to what I see, read and hear are routinely in the form of complaints!

So have I been asking you merely to share the troubles of a long-suffering partner? Not quite. To see why, I need to introduce three additional facts.

First, although the technology is different, many of the formats of popular culture have not changed over centuries. For instance, the people who sought out videos of Saddam Hussein's execution or who glory in the latest exit from the *Big Brother* house may be not be so different from the mob that attended public executions at London's Tyburn in the eighteenth century. Second, the political culture of 'bullshit' and 'spin' that I discuss in Chapter 1 no doubt has many historical parallels as shown by William Hogarth's brilliant cartoons of Georgian London. Third, as my perceptive Editor has pointed out: 'there is nothing uniquely "postmodern" about today's society; if you look back you can say that every age was postmodern to some degree – and equally, like today's society, not postmodern in other respects' (Patrick Brindle, Personal correspondence).

If we accept the validity of the above, and if you are not 'grumpy', 'old' or even a man, what is the relevance of my cultural critique? At its most basic level, I have been suggesting that (what I call) good research, perhaps like good art, in some sense needs to stand outside the taken-for-granted assumptions that inform our everyday life. Put in another word, good research is often counter-cultural.

The aim need not be to criticise the world around us (although it may be) but to allow us a fresh gaze at the way we live. If you return to Michal Chelbin's photographs in Chapter 1, you may get a sense of what I mean.

Throughout this book, I have sought to emphasise that my arguments are unashamedly partial. Many other scholars would resist the answers I offer and even reject the way in which I have posed my questions. I have no problem with that. Nor, if I may say so, should you. My aim will be satisfied if I have managed to involve your interest in a debate. One does not need to be a mystic to believe that setting out on an important journey is, in some respects, more important than arriving at your destination (particularly if that destination is unclear or contested).

A Glossary of Received Ideas

Please note that this contains a list of assumptions and practices that I believe should be avoided. Its aim is to debunk what I take to be conventional assumptions about qualitative research. (Terms in *italic* are cross-referred within this list.)

Access

Qualitative researchers are often troubled by the difficulties of getting access to research sites in order to obtain observational data. This problem trades off a commonsense distinction between the 'inside' and 'outside' of social settings. It is resolvable once we recognise that social phenomena have no 'essential' home. For instance, if we want to study an organisation, publicly available material (e.g. company reports, organisational websites) can be just as relevant as what happens 'inside'.

Anecdotalism

Research reports that appear to tell entertaining stories or anecdotes but fail to provide an analytic or methodological framework with which to convince the reader of their scientific credibility. A common problem in qualitative data reports which appear to choose just those extracts which support the argument being made ('cherry-picking').

Auto-Ethnography

Presenting ethnographic work in the format of a report on one's own personal experiences in the field. 'Rather than seeking primarily to arrive at accurate representations of a common world, the individual turns toward trying to provide honest representations of himself' (Frankfurt, 2005: 65).

Commentary

Interpretations of data which tacitly draw upon commonsense knowledge of social situations and motivations using *undescribed categories,* for example, the common practice of citing certain researcher-relevant categories to describe research subjects (i.e. age, gender, marital status, occupation). These categories implicitly instruct you how to interpret what research subjects say and do. They have an unknown relationship to the categories actually invoked by subjects.

Content analysis

A means of data analysis that establishes a set of categories and then counts the number of instances when those categories are used to describe a particular item of text or an image. Although sometimes treated as a qualitative method, content analysis depends upon the positivist idea of *variables* which are defined at the outset. Content analysis can also deflect you from recognising the sequence within which people organise their accounts.

Divine orthodoxy

An assumption that makes the researcher a kind of philosopher king (or queen) who can always see through people's claims and knows better than they do. The consequence is that practitioners (like doctors or managers) are assumed always to depart from normative standards of good practice.

Experiences

The supposed topic of much qualitative research. In fact, 'experiences' are often treated commonsensically as equivalent to the contents of people's heads and this leads researchers to neglect what people do. 'Experiences' need to be reconceptualised as part of an activity. Telling someone about our experiences is not just emptying out the contents of our head but also organising a tale told to a proper recipient by an authorised teller. In this sense, experiences are 'carefully regulated sorts of things' (Sacks, 1992, 1: 248).

Experimental writing

The abandonment of conventional research reports in favour of poetry or dramatic re-enactments of events (ethnodrama). The problem is that poetry and ethnodrama inhabit a very different world to those worlds (including scientific research as well as courts of law) whose business is making factual claims and where, consequently, some version of 'evidence' matters. Once you discount an appeal to evidence, anything goes (including poetry and ethnodrama).

Explanatory orthodoxy

The assumption that people are puppets of social structures. According to this model, what people do is defined by 'society'. In practice, this reduces to explaining people's behaviour as the outcome of certain *'face-sheet' variables* (like social class, gender or ethnicity). The explanatory orthodoxy is so concerned to rush to an explanation that it fails to ask serious questions about what it is explaining. Its pursuit of 'causes' leads to the neglect of 'what' and 'how' questions (see *Why questions*).

Face-sheet variables

The identity characteristics of individuals (e.g. age, gender, marital status) used by quantitative researchers to explain individuals' perceptions and behaviour. When qualitative researchers invoke such variables (e.g. when they cite such information about interview respondents), they fail to recognise that there are endless ways in which we can describe our identity. When researchers choose particular identity characteristics (say, age and occupation), they ignore how people actively construct identities and move between them. In doing so, they favour particular ways of interpreting what people are saying.

Grand theory

Overarching philosophies or logically-derived accounts of society that generate concepts which often have very little relevance to the practice of qualitative research (e.g. phenomenology, *postmodernism*).

In-depth

The mistaken assumption that qualitative research has the unique ability to go deep inside people's *experiences* (e.g. the claim that 'in-depth interviews represent one of the best possible ways in which to access … experiences, thoughts and opinions' (Sheard, 2011: 623)). Ironically, this is the precise assumption of chatshow hosts and 'psy' professionals (e.g. counsellors, psychotherapists etc.).

Interview society

The way in which many qualitative interviewers tacitly trade off the centrality of the interview format in many contemporary forms of communication. The interview demands subjects who are happy to confess their innermost thoughts and emotions to the appropriate professional. Today the professional who receives their confession is no longer usually a priest but a therapist or media interviewer.

Journalism

For both journalists and many qualitative interviewers, what people tell you is treated as a (more or less accurate) report on people's perceptions of your topic. And instances of what they say can be offered in support of your interpretation (see *Anecdotalism*).

Manufactured data

Data that is a direct artefact of the research process and so would not exist if the researcher were not around (e.g. interviews, focus groups, experiments).

Meanings

Like *experiences*, commonly seen as the main topic of qualitative research. This ignores Max Weber's observation that most social action does not have a fixed 'meaning' attached to it.

Memory

Qualitative researchers seeking accounts of the past can treat 'memory' as something contained inside our heads and therefore 'private' and to be elicited by biographical interviews. This ignores the way in which 'memory' can be interactional. For instance, Sacks invites us to think about those occasions when we had wanted to make a point but the present speaker had continued or someone else had grabbed the floor. In such circumstances, don't we often 'forget' the topic that we wanted to mention? As Sacks observes, 'if you don't get a chance to say it, when you then get a chance to say it, you've forgotten it' (1992, 2: 27). In this respect, memory is not at all private or personal but 'in some perhaps quite dramatic way at the service of the conversation ... It is in some ways an utterance by utterance phenomenon' (1992, 2: 27).

Open-ended interviews

The prescribed format of many qualitative interviews. In order to achieve 'rich data' in the open-ended interview, we are told that the keynote is 'active listening' in which the interviewer 'allows the interviewee the freedom to talk and ascribe meanings' while bearing in mind the broader aims of the project (Noaks and Wincup, 2004: 80). This largely replicates the media's use of the interview for constructing the 'immediate' and 'authentic'. Such an omission fails to recognise that 'interview interactions are inherently spaces in which both speakers are constantly "doing analysis" – both speakers are engaged (and collaborating in) "making meaning" and "producing knowledge"' (Rapley, 2004: 26–7).

Operational definitions

Defining social phenomena at the outset (like Durkheim's initial definition of 'suicide'). A feature of quantitative research which must define its *variables* before measuring them. But such definitions often figure in the way in which qualitative researchers define their research topics and early hypotheses. This can divert us from the study of the organised categories we find in the field and is usually inappropriate to inductive research.

Phenomena escaping

In contemporary culture, the environment around phenomena has become more important than the phenomenon itself. So people tend to be more interested in the lives of movie stars than in the movies themselves. Equally, on sporting occasions, the crowd's Mexican Wave and pre- and post-match interviews with competitors become as exciting (or even more exciting) than the actual game. This has had an unfortunate impact on qualitative research. Because we rush to offer explanations of all kinds of social phenomena, we rarely spend enough time trying to understand how any phenomenon works.

Postmodern research

'An intellectual current characterised by the more-or-less explicit rejection of the rationalist tradition of the Enlightenment, by theoretical discourses disconnected from any empirical test [and] a cognitive and cultural relativism that regards science as nothing more than a 'narration', a 'myth' or a social construction among many others' (Sokal and Bricmont, 1998: 1). 'Postmodern research' can willingly lose contact with claims based on evidence and couched in propositional language. Dressed up in doubtful theoretical verbiage, it not only advocates that 'anything goes' but actually prefers *experimental writing* to clear, refutable statements about research findings.

Romanticism

An approach taken from nineteenth-century thought in which authenticity is attached to personal *experiences*. This is often the approach used in the analysis of interview and focus group data.

Sampling people

A part of a research plan which assumes that, when one is going to do a research study, one always wants to sample 'people' and tends to lead to the pursuit of *manufactured data*. Alternatively, we might sample situations or locations (e.g. internet chatrooms, building design, music lyrics, websites, small ads etc.) and it is then obvious that interviews aren't the only thing to do.

Social problems

The kinds of people, events and situations that are defined as problematic by opinion-formers. Such problems should not usually be used as a resource for a qualitative research topic. By proceeding inductively, we can focus instead on answering the question 'What is going on here?' In this way, we can often come up with findings that are both surprising and useful to participants.

Undescribed categories

When researchers construct *commentaries* on what people say or do, they are working with what Sacks calls 'undescribed categories'. 'To employ an undescribed category is to write descriptions such as appear in children's books. Interspersed with series of words there are pictures of objects' (Sacks, 1963: 7). Instead, we should ask the question 'What work is this account or behaviour doing in just this place?' For instance, the routine positioning of a question like 'What are you doing [on some future date]?' is hearable prior to an invitation.

Variables

Factors that in research are isolated from one another in order to measure the relationship between them (a term usually used only in quantitative research).

Why questions

Questions about causation that are best left to the end of a qualitative research study after we have established how a particular phenomenon is constructed (see *Explanatory orthodoxy*).

Transcription Symbols

[ ]	Brackets: onset and offset of overlapping talk
=	Equal sign: no gap between two utterances
(0.0)	Timed pause: silence measured in seconds and tenths of seconds
(.)	A pause of less than 0.2 seconds
.	Period: falling or terminal intonation
,	Comma: level intonation
?	Question mark: rising intonation
↑	Rise in pitch
↓	Fall in pitch
-	A dash at the end of a word: an abrupt cut-off
<	Immediately following talk is 'jump started', starts with a rush
> <	Faster-paced talk than the surrounding talk
< >	Slower-paced talk than the surrounding talk
____	Underlining: some form of stress, audible in pitch or amplitude
:	Colon(s): prolongation of the immediately preceding sound
° °	Degree signs surrounding a passage of talk: talk with lower volume than the surrounding talk
.hh	A row of 'h's prefixed by a dot: an in-breath
hh	A row of 'h's without a dot: an out-breath
WOrd	Capital letters: utterance, or part thereof, that is spoken much louder than the surrounding talk
(word)	Utterance or part of it in parentheses: uncertainty on the transcriber's part, but a likely possibility
( )	Empty parentheses: something is being said, but no hearing can be achieved
(( ))	Double parentheses: transcriber's descriptions of events, rather than representations of them

Source: adapted by A. Peräkylä from Atkinson and Heritage, 1984

References

Akerstrom, M., Jacobsson, K. and Wasterfors, D. (2004) Reanalysis of previously collected material. In C. Seale, G. Gobo, J. Gubrium and D. Silverman (eds), *Qualitative Research Practice*. London: Sage, 344–58.

Arbus, D. (2005) *Revelations*, Exhibition catalogue. London: Victoria and Albert Museum.

Arendt, H. (1970) Walter Benjamin: 1892–1940. In W. Benjamin, *Illuminations*, tr. H. Zohn. London: Jonathan Cape, 1–58.

Arendt, H. (2006) *Eichmann in Jerusalem: A Report on the Banality of Evil*. London: Penguin Books.

Atkinson, P. and Coffey, A. (2002) Revisiting the relationship between participant observation and interviewing. In J. Gubrium and J. Holstein (eds), *Handbook of Interview Research*. Thousand Oaks, CS: Sage, 801–14.

Atkinson, J.M. and Heritage, J. (eds) (1984) *Structures of Social Action*. Cambridge: Cambridge University Press.

Atkinson, P. and Silverman, D. (1997) Kundera's *Immortality*: the interview society and the invention of self, *Qualitative Inquiry*, 3 (3): 324–45.

Auster, P. (1990) *Moon Palace*, London: Faber and Faber.

Baker, C. (2004) Membership categorization and interview accounts. In D. Silverman (ed.), *Qualitative Research: Theory, Method and Practice* (2nd edn). London: Sage,162–76.

Baker, N. (1997) *The Size of Thoughts*. London: Chatto.

Barnes, J. (2000) *Love etc*. London: Cape.

Becker, H.S. (1998) *Tricks of the Trade: How to Think about your Research while Doing it*. Chicago and London: University of Chicago Press.

Becker, H.S. and Geer, B. (1960) Participant observation: the analysis of qualitative field data. In Adams, R. and Preiss, J. (eds), *Human Organization Research: Field Relations and Techniques*. Homewood, IL: Dorsey.

Beckett, S. (1961/2010) *Happy Days*. London: Faber & Faber.

Bennett, A. (2005) *Untold Stories*. London: Faber & Faber.

Benson, O. and Stangroom, J. (2006) *Why Truth Matters*. London: Continuum.

Bloor, M. (2004) Addressing social problems through qualitative research. In D. Silverman (ed.), *Qualitative Research: Theory, Method and Practice* (2nd edn). London: Sage, 305–24.

Bunting, M. (2010) Increasingly, the rarest experience in family life is undivided attention. *Guardian*, 11 January.

Byrne, B. (2004) Qualitative interviewing. In C. Seale (ed.), *Researching Society and Culture* (2nd edn). London: Sage, 179–92.

Bywater, M. (2007) *Big Babies or: Why Can't We Just Grow Up?* London: Granta Books.

Clavarino, A., Najman, J. and Silverman, D. (1995) Assessing the quality of qualitative data. *Qualitative Inquiry*, 1 (2): 223–42.

Clifford, J. and Marcus, G. (eds) (1986) *Writing Culture*. Berkeley, CA: University of California Press.

Corti, L. and Thompson, P. (2004) Secondary analysis of archived data. In C. Seale, G. Gobo, J. Gubrium and D. Silverman (eds) *Qualitative Research Practice*. London: Sage, 327–43.

Cowan, A. (2006) *What I Know*. London: Sceptre.

Cuff, E.C. and Payne, G.C. (eds) (1979) *Perspectives in Sociology*. London: Allen and Unwin.

Cusk, R. (2007) *Arlington Park*. London: Faber & Faber.

Dalton, M. (1959) *Men Who Manage*. New York: Wiley.

Davenport-Hines, R. (2006) *A Night at the Majestic: Proust and the Great Modernist Dinner Party of 1922*. London: Faber & Faber.

Denzin, N. and Lincoln, Y. (2000) The discipline and practice of qualitative research. In N. Denzin and Y. Lincoln (eds), *Handbook of Qualitative Research* (2nd edn). Thousand Oaks, CA: Sage, 1–28.

Douglas, M. (1975) 'Self-evidence'. In M. Douglas, *Implicit Meanings*. London: Routledge, pp. 276–318.

Drew, P. (1987) Po-faced receipts of teases. *Linguistics*, 25, 219–53.

Drury, M.O.C. (1984) Conversations with Wittgenstein. In R. Rhees (ed.), *Recollections of Wittgenstein*. Oxford University Press: Oxford.

Edwards, D. (1995) Sacks and psychology. *Theory and Psychology*, 5 (3): 579–96.

Emerson, R., Fretz, R. and Shaw, L. (1995) *Writing Ethnographic Fieldnotes*. Chicago, IL: Chicago University Press.

Filmer, P., Phillipson, M., Silverman, D. and Walsh, D. (1972) *New Directions in Sociological Theory*. London: Collier MacMillan.

Flaubert, G. (2005) *Bouvard and Pecuchet*, tr. M. Polizzotti. London: Turnaround.

Flick, U. (1998) *An Introduction to Qualitative Research*. London: Sage.

Flyvbjerg, B. (2004) Five misunderstandings about case-study research. In C. Seale, G. Gobo, J. Gubrium and D. Silverman (eds), *Qualitative Research Practice*. London: Sage, 420–34.

Frankfurt, H.G. (2005) *On Bullshit*. Princeton, NJ: Princeton University Press.

Freebody, P. (2003) *Qualitative Research in Education*, Introducing Qualitative Methods Series. London: Sage.

Fukuyama, F. (2010) *The End of History and the Last Man*. London: Penguin.

Furman, R., Lietz, C. and Langer, C.L. (2006) The research poem in international social work: innovations in qualitative methodology. *International Journal of Qualitative Methods*, 5 (3). Available at www.ualberta.ca/~ijqm/backissues/5_3/html/ furman.htm

Galbraith, J.K. (1999) *The Affluent Society*. London: Penguin.

Garfinkel, E. (1967) *Studies in Ethnomethodology*. Englewood Cliffs, NJ: Prentice-Hall.

Gellner, E. (1975) Ethnomethodology: the re-enchantment industry or a Californian way of subjectivity. *Philosophy of the Social Sciences*, 5 (4): 431–50.

Gergen, K. (1992) Organization theory in the postmodern era. In M. Reed and M. Hughes (eds), *Rethinking Organization: Directions in Organization Theory and Analysis*. London: Sage, 207–226.

Goffman, E. (1959) *The Presentation of Self in Everyday Life*. New York: Doubleday Anchor.

Grey, C. (2005) *A Very Short, Fairly Interesting and Reasonably Cheap Book about Studying Organizations*. London: Sage.

Gubrium, J. (1988) *Analyzing Field Reality*, Qualitative Research Methods Series 8. Newbury Park, CA: Sage.

Gubrium, J. and Holstein, J. (1987) The private image: experiential location and method in family studies. *Journal of Marriage and the Family*, 49: 773–86.

Gubrium, J. and Holstein, J. (eds) (2002) *Handbook of Interview Research*. Thousand Oaks, CA: Sage.

Gubrium, J., Rittman, R., Williams, C., Young, M. and Boylstein, C. (2003) Benchmarking as functional assessment in stroke recovery. *Journal of Gerontology (Social Sciences)*, 58B (4): S203–11.

Hammersley, M. (1992) *What's Wrong with Ethnography?: Methodological Explorations*. London: Routledge.

Hammersley, M. (2004) Teaching qualitative method: craft, profession or bricolage? In C. Seale, G. Gobo, J. Gubrium and D. Silverman (eds) *Qualitative Research Practice*. London: Sage, 549–60.

Heath, C. (1986). *Body. Movement and Speech in Medical Interaction*. Cambridge: Cambridge University Press.

Heath, C. and Luff, P. (2000) *Technology in Action*. Cambridge: Cambridge University Press. Heath, C.C. and Luff, P. (2007) Ordering competition: the interactional accomplishment of the sale of fine art and antiques at auction. *British Journal of Sociology*, 58 (1): 63–85.

Hepburn, A. and Potter, J. (2004) Discourse analytic practice. In C. Seale, G. Gobo, J. Gubrium and D. Silverman (eds), *Qualitative Research Practice*. London: Sage, 180–196.

Heritage, J. (1974) Assessing people. In N. Armistead (ed.), *Reconstructing Social Psychology*. Harmondsworth: Penguin, 260–81.

Heritage, J. (1984) *Garfinkel and Ethnomethodology*. Cambridge: Polity Press.

Heritage, J. and Maynard, D. (2006) Problems and prospects in the study of physician–patient interaction: 30 years of research. *Annual Review of Sociology*, 32, 351–74.

Heritage, J., Robinson, J., Elliott, M., Beckett, M. and Wilkes, M. (2006) Reducing patients' unmet concerns in primary care: a trial of two question designs. Paper presented at the annual meeting of the American Sociological Association, Montreal Convention Center, Montreal, Quebec, Canada, 11 August.

Holstein, J. and Gubrium, J. (1995) *The Active Interview*. Thousand Oaks, CA: Sage.

Holstein, J. and Gubrium, J. (2004) Context: working it up, down and across. In C. Seale, G. Gobo, J. Gubrium and D. Silverman (eds), *Qualitative Research Practice*. London: Sage, 297–311.

Hookway, N. (2008*)* 'Entering the blogosphere': some strategies for using blogs in social research. *Qualitative Research*, 8 (1): 91–113.

Janik, A. and Toulmin, S. (1996) *Wittgenstein's Vienna*. Chicago, IL: Ivan R. Dee.

Jefferson, G. (1973) A case of precision timing in ordinary conversation: overlapped tag-positioned address terms in closing sequences. *Semiotica*, 9(1), 47–96.

Kafka, F. (1961) *Metamorphosis and Other Stories*. Harmondsworth: Penguin.

Kendall, G. and Wickham, G. (1999) *Using Foucault's Methods*, Introducing Qualitative Methods Series. London: Sage.

Ker Muir, Jr., W. (1977) *Police: Streetcorner Politicians*. Chicago, IL: University of Chicago Press.

Koppel, R. (2005) Role of computerized physician order entry systems in facilitating medical errors. *Journal of American Medical Association*, 293 (10): 1197–1202.

Kozinets, R.V. (2010) *Netnography: Doing Ethnographic Research Online*. London: Sage.

Kundera, M. (1989) *Immortality*. London: Faber & Faber.

Kundera, M. (2000) *Immortality*. London: Faber & Faber.

Kundera, M. (2004) *The Unbearable Lightness of Being*. New York: Harper Collins.

Kunzru, H. (2011) Postmodernism: from the cutting edge to the museum. *Guardian* (Review), 17 September, 18–19.

Lanzmann, C. (Dir.) (1985) *Shoah*. French documentary film. New Yorker Films.

Lehman, D. (1991) *Signs of the Times*. London: Andre Deutsch.

Levi, P. (1979) *If This Is a Man*. London: Penguin.

Linstead, A. and Thomas, H. (2002) 'What do you want from me?' A poststructuralist feminist reading of middle managers' identities. *Culture and Organization*, 8 (1):1–20.

Macnaghten, P. and Myers, G. (2004) Focus groups. In C. Seale, G. Gobo, J. Gubrium and D. Silverman (eds), *Qualitative Research Practice*. London: Sage, 65–79.

Markham, A.N. (2011) Internet research. In D. Silverman (editor) *Qualitative Research*. London: Sage, 111–28.

Maynard, D. (1991) Interaction and asymmetry in clinical discourse. *American Journal of Sociology*, 97 (2): 448–95.

Maynard, D. (2003) *Bad News, Good News: Conversational Order in Everyday Talk and Clinical Settings*. Chicago, IL: Chicago University Press.

McLeod, J. (1994) *Doing Counselling Research*. London: Sage.

Miller, G. and Fox, K. (2004) Building bridges: the possibility of analytic dialogue between ethnography, conversation analysis and Foucault. In D. Silverman (editor), *Qualitative Research: Theory, Method and Practice*. London: Sage, 35–55.

Miller, G., Dingwall, R. and Murphy, E. (2004) Using qualitative data and analysis: reflections on organizational research. In D. Silverman (editor), *Qualitative Research: Theory, Method and Practice*. London: Sage, 325–41.

Moerman, M. (1974) Accomplishing ethnicity. In R. Turner (ed.) *Ethnomethodology*. Harmondsworth: Penguin, 54–68.

Moerman, M. and Sacks, H. (1971) On Understanding in Conversation, unpublished paper, 70th Annual Meeting, American Anthropological Association, New York City, 20 November.

Moisander, J. and Valtonen, A. (2006) *Qualitative Marketing Research: A Cultural Approach*. London: Sage.

Nadai, E. and Maeder, C. (2006) The promises and ravages of performance: enforcing the entrepreneurial self in welfare and economy. Summary of the Project No. 4051–69081 National Research Program 51 'Social Integration and Social Exclusion' (www.nfp51.ch). Olten, Switzerland: Olten & Kreuzlingen.

Noaks, L. and Wincup, E. (2004) *Criminological Research: Understanding Qualitative Methods*. London: Sage.

O'Neill, M., in association with S. Giddens, P. Breatnach, C. Bagley, D. Bourne and T. Judge (2002) Renewed methodologies for social research: ethno-mimesis as performative praxis. *The Sociological Review*, 50 (1): 69.

Orr, J. (1996) *Talking About Machines: An Ethnography of a Modern Job*. Ithaca, NY: Cornell University Press.

Pascal, F. (1984) Wittgenstein: a personal memoir. In R. Rhees (ed.), *Recollections of Wittgenstein*. Oxford and New York: Oxford University Press.

Peräkylä, A. (1995) *AIDS Counselling*. Cambridge: Cambridge University Press.

Peräkylä, A., Ruusuvuori, J. and Vehviläinen, S. (2005) Introduction: professional theories and institutional interaction. *Communication and Medicine*, 2 (2): 105–10.

Percy, W. (2002) The loss of the creature. In D. Bartholomae and A. Petrosky (eds), *Ways of Reading: an Anthology for Writers*. New York: St. Martin's, 588–601.

Pinter, H. (1976) *Plays: One*. London: Methuen.

Polyani, M. (1964) *Personal Knowledge: Towards a Post-Critical Philosophy*. New York: Harper & Row.

Popper, K. (1976) Reason or revolution? In T.W. Adorn, H. Albert, R. Dahrendorf, J. Habermas, H. Pilot and K. Popper (eds), *The Positivist Dispute in German Sociology*. London: Heinemann, 288–300.

Porter, H. (1995) Gee, if you wanna talk about it Hugh. *Guardian*, 29 June.

Potter, J. (1996) Discourse analysis and constructionist approaches: theoretical background. In J. Richardson (ed.) *Handbook of Qualitative Research Methods for Psychology and the Social Sciences*, Leicester: BPS Books, 125–40.

Potter, J. (2002) Two kinds of natural. *Discourse Studies*, 4 (4): 539–42.

Potter, J. (2004) Discourse analysis as a way of analysing naturally-occurring talk. In D. Silverman (editor), *Qualitative Research: Theory, Method and Practice*. London: Sage, 200–21.

Potter, J. and Hepburn, A. (2007) Life is out there: a comment on Griffin. *Discourse Studies*, 9 (2): 276–82.

Puchta, C. and Potter, J. (2004) *Focus Group Practice*. London: Sage.

Rapley, T. (2004) Interviews. In C. Seale, G. Gobo, J. Gubrium and D. Silverman (eds), *Qualitative Research Practice*. London: Sage, 15–33.

Roth, P. (2006) *Everyman*. London: Jonathan Cape.

Sacks, H. (1963) Sociological description. *Berkeley Journal of Sociology*, 8: 1–16.

Sacks, H. (1972) Notes on police assessment of moral character. In D. Sudnow (ed.), *Studies in Social Interaction*. New York: Free Press, 280–93.

Sacks, H. (1987) On the preferences for agreement and contiguity in sequences in conversation. In G. Button and J.R.E. Lee (eds), *Talk and Social Organization*. Clevedon, Philadelphia: Multilingual Matters, 54–69. (From a lecture by H.Sacks (1970), edited by E. Schegloff.)

Sacks, H. (1992) *Lectures on Conversation* (2 volumes), edited by Gail Jefferson with an Introduction by Emmanuel Schegloff. Oxford: Blackwell. [*Note:* page references in the text refer to each volume in the following format: Volume 1 (1:345) Volume 2 (2:345).]

Sacks, H., Schegloff, E.A. and Jefferson, G. (1974) A simplest systematics for the organization of turn-taking in conversation. *Language*, 50 (4): 696–735.

Saunders, F.S. (2011) Don't give me grief. *Guardian* (Review), 20 August.

Saussure, F. de (1974) *Course in General Linguistics*. London: Fontana.

Schegloff, E.A. (1968) Sequencings in conversational openings. *American Anthropologist*, 70: 1075–95.

Schegloff, E.A. (1991) Reflections on talk and social structure. In D. Boden and D. Zimmerman (eds), *Talk and Social Structure: Studies in Ethnomethodology and Conversation Analysis*. Cambridge: Polity Press, 44–70.

Schegloff, E. and Sacks, H. (1974) Opening up closings. In R. Turner (ed.), *Ethnomethodology*. Harmondsworth: Penguin, 233–64.

Schon, D. (1983) *The Reflective Practitioner*. London: Temple Smith.

Seale, C. (2011) Secondary analysis of qualitative data. In D. Silverman (ed.) *Qualitative Research*. London: Sage, 347–64.

Shaw, R. and Kitzinger, C. (2005) Calls to a homebirth help line: empowerment in childbirth. *Social Science and Medicine*, 61: 2374–83.

Sheard, L. (2011) 'Anything could have happened': women, the night-time economy, alcohol and drink spiking. *Sociology*, 49 (4): 619–33.

Silverman, D. (1968) Clerical ideologies: a research note. *British Journal of Sociology*, XIX, 3: 326–33.

Silverman, D. (1970) *The Theory of Organizations*. London: Heinemann (New York: Basic Books, 1971).

Silverman, D. (1987) *Communication and Medical Practice*. London: Sage.

Silverman, D. (1997) *Discourses of Counselling: HIV Counselling as Social Interaction*. London: Sage.

Silverman, D. (1998) *Harvey Sacks and Conversation Analysis*, Polity Key Contemporary Thinkers Series. Cambridge: Polity Press (New York: Oxford University Press).

Silverman, D. (2010) *Doing Qualitative Research: A Practical Handbook* (3rd edn). London: Sage.

Silverman, D. (ed.) (2011) *Qualitative Research* (3rd edn). London: Sage.

Silverman, D. (2012) *Interpreting Qualitative Data* (4th edn). London: Sage.

Silverman, D. and Gubrium, J. (1994) Competing strategies for analyzing the contexts of social interaction. *Sociological Inquiry*, 64 (2): 179–98.

Silverman, D. and Jones, J. (1976) *Organizational Work: The Language of Grading/The Grading of Language*. London: Collier-MacMillan.

Silverman, D. and Torode, B. (1980) *The Material Word: Some Theories of Language and its Limits*. London: Routledge.

Sokal, A. and Bricmont, J. (1998) *Intellectual Impostures*. London: Profile.

Speer, S. (2002) 'Natural' and 'contrived' data: a sustainable distinction? *Discourse Studies*, 4 (4): 511–25.

Sudnow, D. (1968) *Passing On: The Social Organization of Dying*. Englewood Cliffs, NJ: Prentice-Hall.

Sullivan, M. (1993) Ethnodrama and reality: commentary on the house that crack built. The American Prospect, 1 January.

Waitzkin, H. (1979) 'Medicine, Superstructure and Micropolitics', *Social Science and Medicine*, 13A, 601–609.

Weber, M. (1949) *Methodology of the Social Sciences*. New York: Free Press.

Wilkinson, S. and Kitzinger, C. (2000) Thinking differently about thinking positive: a discursive approach to cancer patients' talk. *Social Science and Medicine*, 50: 797–811.

Wittgenstein, L. (1980) *Culture and Value*. Oxford: Blackwell.

Author Index

Subject Index